Treasured

The truth about your worth and value

By

MIRACLE REED

Feat. The Treasured Girls

ISBN-13: 978-0-9904779-2-1 (paperback)
ISBN-13: 978-0-9904779-3-8 (eBook)

CONTENTS

LET GO AND LET LOVE FLOW

ENDORSEMENTS

Treasured is a must read for any woman who has ever felt broken or out of place. *Treasured* cuts through the ludicrous lies the world has told women from the beginning of time, and with the soft and loving voice of a sister provides biblical and real world examples on how to build any broken, incomplete, or uncertain woman back up to wholeness. Miracle Reed, through The Holy Spirit's direction, lifts the burden of responsibility of being "good enough" off of every woman's shoulders by simply showing her she was made to be MORE THAN ENOUGH! This I not a book to pass on! It is a manual for success, and survival for today's modern woman!"

Lady Fran Reid-Barnes
The Well Kept Woman, CEO & Designer

Treasured was heaven to my mind, body, and soul. It could not have come at a more perfect time as a mother of a teenage daughter that just begun her high school career. I've been focused on keeping her grounded in the word of the Lord. We read this book together and was inspired by God's destiny for Nia. Thank you Pastor Miracle for your exceptional gift of teaching the Word.

Love Always,

Karida Green and Nia Hamilton
Mother and Daughter

What a breath of fresh air Miracle Reed's *Treasured* book is for this generation of young women. The biblical principles she shares are uniquely woven to bring fullness of life! Women of all ages will also find this book inspiring to be discussed, taught, and shared with one another and with the young women in their lives. This book is so biblically sound, and it brings many wonderful tools for young women to use and stand firm on. It is a necessary word of truth to come against the onslaught of a culture spinning out of control. As a former teacher and minister to hundreds of teenage girls, I highly recommend *Treasured* to every young woman in America who wants to walk with integrity, character, and the assurance that she is *Treasured* by the One that matters most.

Luanne Botta
Speaker/Author

First, I want to thank Miracle Reed for being such a light to the World, and for blessing me with the honor of reading and endorsing this book called *Treasured* before it is published. Her name is a true testament to the ministry God works through her. She is truly called by God to be a blessing to others for Jesus. This book will help light the path to find your identity in Christ as Miracle takes you on a real journey of finding the 100% authentic you. If you struggle with feelings of insecurity, depression, peer pressure, suicide, or feeling the need to measure up to the world's standards, then this book is for you. You may not have any of these issues I mentioned, but I believe if you read this book you will find out more about who you are as a woman of God. Take the journey, and find the real you!

Jonique Waiters
Church: Trinity Fellowship International
Leader of Women Joined Together in Faith Out Reach Ministry

I thoroughly enjoyed reading *Treasured*. Young ladies in this day and age are so fortunate to have an author who will speak the truth in love, covering ground that, when I was a young girl, no one had talked about. From the honor and privilege of living totally surrendered to Jesus, to consequences of living life our own way, yet explaining the opportunity we have to always begin again. This is a book I will keep for my granddaughter to read because it sums up what I want her to know about her value and worth in the eyes of God, God's love toward her, and the priceless treasure she truly is, a DOTK. Especially in this day and age where the word of the world is so contrary to the Word of God. As a wife and mother, this book is a great reminder for me to enjoy this particular moment in time, the place where God has me, and not try to rush through life. I really enjoyed the input from the *Treasured Girls*. And now I know why Miracle loves her pearls!

Mrs. Sheila Rivers
Certified Biblical Counselor
Registered Professional Court Reporter
DOTK!

I now understand why Miracle wears pearls.

An oyster, to protect itself from irritation, will quickly begin covering any uninvited visitor in its shell with layers of a protective coating called nacre. Layer upon layers of this protective coating surrounds the irritant until the pearl is formed.

God is forming us into a hidden treasure by covering us with Himself. Like a pearl, His protective coating helps protect us while forming us into a jewel. Miracle's book will encourage you and add another layer of protection around God's hidden gem. It will guide you to trust God to be your nacre, to allow Him to protect you from all irritants. To enable you to be formed into whom God created you to be - a Daughter of the King.

Veronica Saul - Friend
Youth Ministry, Hart Pentecostal Church
Prince George, British Columbia

FOREWORD

There is a quiet beauty found in the making of a pearl that is unparalleled to any gemstone because of its *process of becoming known*. Its life begins with languish, being weakened in an oysters case by happenstance—a modicum of sand implants itself in the oyster as a foreign object and the oyster begins to secrete nacre for protection. You may be thinking to yourself, "How does something so exquisite begin its life by having to protect itself?" Well, if you wait a few years, you'll learn that from a pearl's beginning emerges a marvelous work. The nacre (the source of protection) is nothing less than the result of the encasing of crystals that forms the *beauty* of a pearl. Now, you can take a deep breath of relief. God is in the process of creating a pearl of you, but it won't be by happenstance!

Miracle Reed, my sister, is inviting you into her *process of becoming known* the pearl spoken of. Mankind is unable to naturally recreate the phenomenon of a pearl; this uniqueness is without a doubt emanated through the lens of

Miracle's life. She was declared dead (weakened) at birth, then her encasing commenced with God's hand literally forming this beautiful tapestry of life—*A Pearl.* Even through her brokenness, like a pearl, Miracle was introduced to the world, as complete. Her Father God made her whole, a single anomaly for no other gemstone can be presented without being cut or polished to bring forth *beauty*, but a pearl.

Treasured appeals to the pearl crystallizing from out of you. You will find an anthology of stories told by ladies who've encountered challenges in life encased by Miracle's enlightened message of Hope. There is no hidden agenda in this book. In true Miracle fashion, she offers practical "how to" instructions germane to the life of many women. It will be like looking into a pond of your reflection but providing a hopeful outlook to your future. The author makes herself available to you as her own testimony unveils how God has brought new meaning to her life.

As a woman of candor, Miracle pieces a message of directness. There is a sense of gentle urgency to the words inked on each page. Because of her undeniable trust in God, each word written is also lifted up as a prayer for the lady reading this book. She believes in God's **right now** miracles, healing, and restoration. The boldness of her approach to providing practical insights for life changing outcomes derives from her confidence in the power of the Holy Spirit. To Miracle, there is no believing a lie of an overreliance on God for she surrenders her life, her daily thoughts - even you - to God. She is result-driven because she knows God's Word is promising. When encapsulated by God's forming hand, Miracle challenges the pearl in you to be made known by HIM. She includes the testimony of ladies so that their tapestry of light can capture someone's life just as her life does for many. Her message is to be a billboard for Christ; an ambassador of His love.

In a world where mediocrity is ubiquitous, the author challenges you to develop a robust faith towards a life of excellence. Her message brilliantly illustrates the love of the Supreme Father for His treasured daughters. Her message reminds you that you are still daddy's little girl, and He is holding your hand through your tough times. It's so inspiring to hear a comforting voice telling you, "I am carrying you, my daughter," as you read the words in this book. Miracle assures you that you are accepted in a world that rejects spiritual excellence. She invites you to take charge of your life!

I am giddy about your encounter with God as you hold this book in your hands because this **WILL BE** intimate. Irrespective of where you are in life, *Treasured* meets you with a message to strengthen your walk with Christ or to develop a relationship that you've never known. Listen to the whispers of the ebbing ocean tides, you are the pearl *becoming known* by HIM. It is my prayer that this book awakens the treasured pearl from within you.

— Karlin Larkin

INTRODUCTION

It wasn't too long ago that I was the girl, unhappy, complacent with mediocrity and wishing I looked different. I recall asking God why I looked the way I did. I couldn't figure out why everyone else around me possessed a beauty that I felt I was certainly missing. From wanting a nose job, different hair, and lighter skin complexion, one thing was sure: I had no clue of who I was. It wasn't long before I envied the outward appearances of friends and other people who had what I felt was missing in me. I would even practice making certain facial expressions in the mirror so that my nose or cheek bones would look different. The truth of the matter is, I spent so much time looking at the outward aspect of beauty rather than paying attention to what God said about me.

You see, we all have those moments when we look at who we are or who we have become and find ourselves going on a downward spiral of insecurity. It only takes that one friend, relationship, job, coworker, one university or church experience, to change everything. However, while I have had my fair share of circumstances in life that have not always been positive; what I have come to realize is that life and our identity should never be based on what we have experienced, but rather how we choose to *respond*. We can't always control what happens, but we can control how we react to various circumstances in our lives. I am no different from you. I spent many years of my life reaching for levels of achievement, relationships, and an identity that would give me some degree of confidence; only to find that what I desired the most would ultimately come from God. As ladies coming from various socioeconomic backgrounds, family dynamics, and ages we have a variety of experiences that can either distract us from being all that we can be or challenge us to become the very best. However, what we make of these experiences, one way or the other, is up to us.

I knew that I could either allow my family dynamics to stay in dysfunction, or I could allow the love of God to flow through me, allowing me to be a change agent. I knew that I could either wallow in sorrow because of a nine-year relationship that ended, or I could literally find empowerment like never before in my season of singleness. I could take advantage of the opportunities because of the new experiences and friendships that were coming my way. However, I chose to look at life not based on the circumstances that had taken place, but rather my view, my interpretation, and my decision to find joy in the consistency of God. With that, I began to search the scriptures and took a look at what God said about me. What I found was that what He said about me in the Bible and what I was saying about myself were two different things. Does this sound familiar? While I was looking at what was external and fleeting, God was inviting me on a journey to understand who I was in Him. It wasn't long before I started to look in the mirror and no longer criticized everything that I saw. However, I didn't say that I wasn't still struggling with criticizing myself, I just didn't criticize *everything* that I saw. I began to see that there was more to me than what I ever could've imagined. Choosing to identify yourself according to God's perspective is a very different experience than looking through the lens that we have created for ourselves.

In fact, there is no real way to see the authentic you without seeking God authentically for yourself. Sure, there may be other things that motivate you to seek God. But, to know who you really are, you must know who He really is. God created you with purpose, and that purpose has very little - if anything at all - to do with the color of your hair, the arch of your eyebrows, shape of your eyes, or how straight your teeth may or may not be. These are outward factors by which the world measures beauty, but not what God acknowledges or deems of great value or significance. According to 1 Samuel 16:17, "… People judge by outward appearance, but the Lord looks at the heart." How refreshing is that?! God is not looking at what took you two hours to do, He is looking at what took you only moments to decide. In other words, God is more interested in your decision of choosing Him than your choice of clothes or foundation for the day.

Understanding your worth and value and actually believing it for yourself are two entirely different things. This is a process that you have to be open to. No one can make you feel good about who you are, it comes from choosing to see how God sees you. Sure, people will give compliments and even flatter you from time to time, but your identity and worth will never be validated in those terms. As you seek God and ask Him for His "eyes" to properly see you, I believe you will be blown away. The magnitude of your beauty, worth, and value is far more than what the human eye can perceive. May you have a heart that is open to receive all that God has in store for you!

You see, as daughters of the King you must realize that who you are - and *whose* you are - is far greater than what you have. Your worth is not measured by anything that an attractive guy may say or the amount of people who admire you; it is measured by the content of your character. I'm sure you've met people whom you thought were gorgeous, attractive, fine, etc., but when you've gotten to know them, you found that their personality or character was not as appealing. I would imagine that you probably grew tired of their personality and maybe even stopped spending time with them because of it. We must be reminded that, while *beauty may capture the eye, your character is what captures the heart.*

Do you know that today there are reality TV shows that have the power to change everything from your eyebrows, wardrobe and even the way you walk, but having no impact on your negative character or personality? That's right! We live in a society that is obsessed with maintaining a counterfeit appearance of beauty, while never dealing with the issues of the heart. You can be gorgeous and have a terrible personality, ultimately causing you to be viewed in a negative way. Everything on the outside can be fixed up, glammed up, and "on fleek"; but if the inside has not been transformed by Jesus Christ, the beauty outwardly adored is nothing more than a mask. I don't know about you, but I want to know when I have traded in the beauty of God's creation for a mask that has been created by man.

The origin of this book came from a home group that I was leading for teen girls while living in Canada. After hearing many of these teens share how they felt about themselves, social media, and boys, I felt a strong need to help in establishing fundamental principles of worth and value for them. In doing this, I invited all of the girls who wanted to have a part in this book to share what the phrase "I am treasured" meant to them and a scripture that they felt helped them see who they were in God. You will hear from these girls throughout this book and how God has shown them who they really are. There will be chapters throughout the book that will open your mind to the worth and value that you have as a daughter of the King as well as chapters that will challenge you to let go of the limits that you've placed on your life.

It is my hope and prayer that you are encouraged and uplifted in your life and that you are able to see who you really are in God. I know that TV, social media, and entertainment have a way of redefining what beauty is, but believe not what you see, believe only what God has made clear in His Word. His Word - the Bible - is the only truth and standard by which one can truly succeed, live a life of joy, and a life of complete wholeness. God made you complete, and He made you to stand out, don't search for ways to fit in. May you open up your mind to a new way of thinking about yourself and may you speak life over yourself, declaring, "I am treasured."

CHAPTER 1

"Just Be You"

"I praise you because I am fearfully and wonderfully made; your works are wonderful; I know that full well." Psalm 139:14 (NIV)

Do you know that the most beautiful gift you could ever give someone is the 100% authentic you? It's true, no one can be a better you. No one can do what you can do, the way you can do it. In fact, God has specifically created you unique and different from every other person walking on the face of the earth. How amazing is that?! There is no one like you. While you are trying to imitate or mold yourself into someone who you are not, people are waiting for the real you to be revealed. Some girls have stories much like your own: feelings of insecurity, depression, peer pressure, even suicide. Do you know the root cause of all of these negative things? It's the lie of "perfection." It's this lie that keeps every girl convinced that she is not sufficient enough.

It is the same lie that convinces us, as girls, to believe that we will never measure up to the world's standard of beauty.

The reality is, no one on this earth is perfect. Those we perceive as perfect, aren't perfect either. Why? Because we haven't spent enough time with these people to be made aware of their flaws or have never met them in person. Our desire as DOTK (Daughters of the King) should be to live our lives understanding that our worth isn't measured by how we look, what people say about us, or what we may think of ourselves. Our goal is to be a walking billboard of God's perfect love in our lives. You are never more beautiful then when you see yourself – your true beauty - through God's eyes. That's right! People can tell you, your family can tell you, and you can even be voted prom queen, but if you do not see your true beauty for yourself, none of these things matter. You are a diamond in the rough, and the process of having a brilliant shine is being able to see past the rough (the imperfections, the other girls, the pictures, social media, etc.).

The truth is, you could never shine brighter than when you allow God's love to shine through you. You don't shine or stand out because of the new outfit, perfectly straight teeth after wearing braces, or the length of your hair; it's God who shines through you. When you are able to see how fearfully and wonderfully made you really are, you will begin to see that you have so much more to offer than what you think. You probably know people who are struggling with their image, but can I challenge and encourage you to read over Psalm 139:14 and make it your declaration as you share it with your friends? There is power in the declared Word of God, your life will be changed and the way you view yourself will be transformed!

Notice that David states in the Book of Psalms that not only are we fearfully and wonderfully made, but he also highlights our ability to know it *full well*. This means that we have the potential to know with our whole heart who we are in God and can live a life that is reflective of what God says about us. I know that at this point in your life you have been told many things, you have said many things, and you have believed many things that are not true. But God is able to restore (make up for) the time that you've spent believing those things. Today you can make the decision to take a stand and to hold on to God's Word. When He looks at you, He calls you precious and declares that you are His daughter.

It may be hard for you to see yourself as a daughter if you have not had a positive relationship with your father, or maybe have never met your father, but that does not mean that God cannot give you the love that you need as His daughter. You don't have to spend your life worried about God letting you down, missing your birthday, or not treating you right. God desires to be all that you could ever need or want. He loves you with an everlasting love. God does not love you because of all that you do right or not love you because of what you do wrong, He loves you completely and unconditionally; no matter the day and no matter the situation, He loves you!

Maybe you think to yourself, "Of course God will love me no matter what I look like, but the world will not." Do you know that according to Romans 12:2, you are not a part of the world or its views? You have a much higher standard to live by; it's called "Kingdom Living" (living according to the King, the Word of God). Therefore, no matter what the world thinks of you; you do not belong to this world, you belong to the KING. You see, the world is also searching for acceptance and truth, just like you are searching for the very same thing. However, only the one who seeks God will actually find it. Your beauty is not found at the MAC Cosmetics counter or at the mall, it is found in God. When you seek Him, you will find true beauty from within.

One of the most challenging things to do today is to actually be honest about who you are. If there is one thing that most of society is running from, it is authenticity. From make-up commercials to the new workout fad, everyone is searching outside of who they are to become who they are not. I'm not saying that there is something wrong with trying to correct areas of your life that are a result of poor choices, but when we seek for approval from others as a result of what we've done for ourselves, we are being motivated by the wrong things. When a decision is made on the foundation of insecurity or fear of rejection, nothing good or lasting will come from it.

For us to really know who we are, we must accept who we are not, without the thought of who would accept us if certain things were different. The love that God gives freely is not because of what we've changed or altered, it's given because we stand in need of love that is not conditionally measured. We all stand in need of love that is not driven by performance or gain; this is what God freely gives to us. When we search for love and acceptance from people as an attempt to feel better about ourselves, we rob them of the real us and we miss out on real and authentic encounters with others. You see, it's not the people around us who stand in the way of us being comfortable in our own skin, it's the lies that we've believed about ourselves that do.

I remember battling as a teenager with insecurity and seeing other girls - and even now in my adult years as well - who I thought were more gorgeous than me. I would constantly compare myself to what I saw in those people. In many ways, I would criticize myself and try to figure out in what ways I could change all of the things that I didn't like. Do you know what I came to realize? I came to realize that it wasn't all of the things about myself that I didn't like, it was me, myself that I didn't like. The truth is, when you are not content with who you are as a person, you will not be content with hardly anything about yourself. I soon realized that the problem was not my nose or eyebrows. The root of the problem was that I did not see myself in the image and likeness of God.

You see, when we measure our value by the world's standards we neglect the beauty of the Creator. Being made in His image and in His likeness (Genesis 1:27), we must acknowledge that God knew exactly what He was doing, and there are no mistakes. We must learn that what we admire about another should not turn into a criticism of what we do not like about ourselves. We have a hard time in this area because usually seeing something in another person that we like, often points to some sort of difference or flaw that we recognize in ourselves. Can I ask you this: Can what you lack (in your opinion) actually be a flaw because it's being measured by the standard of another and not the original intent of the Creator? I would think that it can't in many ways. Who you really are is who God intended you to be. In fact, your real life is not actually lived out until you see it through the eyes of God (Colossians 3:3).

"Just be You"

You have not actually experienced life until you've truly experienced God. When you do, you will know it and if you have, you already know the truth of this declaration. Being comfortable with who you are is being able to see areas of improvement in your life and not think any more or any less of yourself based on those areas of improvement. When you are able to do that, you're headed in the right direction. Finding joy in knowing that you are who you are because God is who He is, gives everything else in our lives perspective. When we lose sight of that, we are bound to lose sight of the bigger things.

In this opening chapter make the decision to take off the mask, to remove the shield, and to just be you. You have more to offer than you think, and more people admire you just the way you are than you could ever have imagined. Don't allow the real you to be hidden in an attempt to protect yourself from what you've created in your mind. This; the perfected state of you, will be produced only in the full state of Christ in you. This means that the perfect image of yourself can only be found in Christ, and actually has nothing to do with the image that you've conjured up in your mind.

The Lie of Perfection usually follows this pattern; "If only I had this, wore this, done this, said that, lived there, been there, seen them, and spoke to her, then I would be perfect." But let me tell you, my sister, that this is indeed a lie. There is nothing and no one who can make you perfect but God Himself. And even in God making you perfect in your own sight, it's actually not you, but Christ who has been welcomed into your heart doing the heavy lifting. Perfection is not a state of being, it is a state of mind, and that mind must be renewed daily (Romans 12:2). Every day the Enemy (Satan) wants you to focus on what you don't have, instead of having a spirit of thankfulness and humility for what God has given you. So, when the trap of perfection comes, remind yourself of who lives in your heart.

The real you is dying to come out, to be seen, to no longer be hidden. Deep down, I believe that you no longer desire to be hidden. Allow me to encourage you; you don't have to run from who you are anymore. You aren't the only one who has experienced a bad hair day, family crisis, acne breakout, job loss or financial crisis. Many girls are going through the exact same thing, and you know what that is? It's called life! This is a part of your journey and how you choose to respond to how you feel will ultimately be the defining factor of your life. I promise that life will not end because of what happened yesterday, who ignored you the day before, or your size. Your life is more precious and valuable than all of those things. In fact, nothing here on earth can measure your beauty.

Be you without making excuses. Be you without feeling guilty. Be you without feeling awkward. Be you when you feel like running and hiding the most. Be you because people need *you*.

Be you because the most beautiful person you could ever be is you. Everything and everyone else is counterfeit. Choose you.

CHAPTER 2

"Be Strong and Laugh"

"She is clothed with strength and dignity, and she
laughs without fear of the future."
Proverbs 31:25 (NLT)

This verse has played a huge part in my life over the last couple of years. I have been through quite a bit, but I always returned to this verse. There are an endless number of reasons to why I chose to share this verse with you, but the main reason is that I firmly believe that all girls can relate to it, in one way or another. When it says, "She is clothed in strength," the first thing that comes to my mind is that I am covered in Gods' strength, not only in trials and tribulations but every single minute of every single day. Not only are you covered in His strength, but His unfailing love and mercy as well. God loves you despite your past or what you've done. Let go of the fear that you are holding onto. Whether it is a fear of not being good enough, not pleasing everyone, failing to provide for your family or even the fear of what your future holds. Fear is the devil's way of getting to you. God has you in his mighty hands. YOU are worthy of so much more and God is just waiting to blow you away. It's time for you to let go of what is holding you back and start living your life. You are treasured. Laugh without fear of the future because you have nothing to worry about. God has a plan for you—you just have to believe it.

Alexis Mcmordie, Treasured Girl

How encouraging is it to hear these very words from Alexis? Not only does God care about you, but He also cares about your future and the decisions you make today that play a significant role in your tomorrow. According to the scripture above, the woman is clothed with strength and dignity. This is a part of the woman's apparel. Everything that you are able to do will be done according to the apparel that you put on. You see, we make a daily choice to clothe ourselves in that which brings life or that which brings death. Our choice is often based on how we feel from day to day and the experiences that we are choosing to maximize in our perception. However, if we take in what Alexis has shared about our knowledge that our strength comes from God, we will easily see that who we are is identified in who we allow God to be in our lives.

Maybe you read what Alexis said and thought to yourself, "I will never be able to walk in freedom and not have fear about my future because of the things that I've gone through." Allow me to encourage you, your future is not defined by what you've gone through but how you came out on the other side. You can either spend your life held back, or you can spend your life empowered by all of the things that have tried to hold you back! The truth is that no matter how bad your past was, it's in the past, and it does not have to determine your present or your future. There is a fantastic plan that God has for your life, and the moment you begin to identify yourself by His plan and not your thoughts, *that* is the moment that you will experience freedom.

It may seem impossible to you right now, but you can be like the woman that Proverbs 31 is referring to. You can be the woman that laughs without fear of the future. Sure, you will have days when you doubt yourself but don't stay in that doubt. At times, the reality of freedom will seem too good to be true, but don't question it. In fact, when in doubt, run! Your future is secure with God, and the plan that He has for you is without flaw or error. Rest in the assurance of God's promise to you that He will never leave nor forsake you, even in the times when you feel like giving up on yourself. Dare to believe that God will provide you with the greatest life that you could ever live. Dare to trust Him with your whole heart and allow God to heal you from what people have said, things that have happened, and negative decisions you have made.

Don't allow people and experiences that have brought hurt to your life to prevent you from moving forward. You have the ability to take control over the negative thoughts that enter your mind, and you have the ability to choose what defines you. God certainly has a plan for your life, and that plan is to give you a fantastic future (Jeremiah 29:11). That's right, God desires to give you an amazing future that will rely less on you and more on Him. Sure, you can try to make some things happen for yourself, but ultimately your life and success rests in God. *True success is what is done for God, submitted to God, and made available by God.* Keep in mind that people cannot stand in the way of what God is doing unless you give them the power to do so. Take the authority away from your peers, and ask God to help you place your time, effort, and attention what His purpose is for you. You may even have to consider how the opinions of people became such a priority in your life.

Have you ever asked yourself, "Why do I care so much about what people think of me or about the things that happened in my past?" Have you ever found solid answers for either of these questions? If you haven't, it may be because the truth is found in what we usually don't want to see. What that means is, we have given people and circumstances too much power over us. Sure, we may not want to admit it, but most of the time, our problem is not that we haven't taken control of our lives, but that we have given the power to our peers or to our problems. Just think of how often you've decided not to wear your hair a certain way or put on a particular dress because of the fear of what others may think or say. At that moment, you have willingly given your strength, your ability to choose, and your value to someone other than God. This will always leave you feeling weak because the one who has the power to strengthen you has been neglected.

As a young woman, I have slowly learned the importance and power of my words. I began to realize that I would never understand my worth and value as a DOTK if my words did not match what I was trying to believe about myself. Maybe you are finding the same thing to be true for you. Maybe you want to believe that you are treasured and valued by God, but for some reason, your words are not lining up. This may come as a shock to you, but the reality is that whatever is in your heart, at some point, will show its face. According to Luke 6:45, out of the abundance of the heart, the mouth speaks. No matter how often we may try to camouflage our feelings - deep down inside - they can't be escaped. When you really begin to see that you have value in God and in this world (because of your role in building God's Kingdom), you will start to declare it. You will begin to believe it, and more importantly, you will start to live it.

When you begin to realize that it's the enemy's goal to keep you stuck and weak, you will automatically begin to look for opportunities for empowerment. These opportunities are challenges turned into victories. These opportunities are moments of defeat turned into moments of celebration. Every circumstance that has the potential of robbing you of your strength and your laugh are opportunities that you can use as tools of empowerment. You may look at people and think that they have it all together, but everyone has a story. Everyone has had battles that they have had to fight, withstand, and made a decision to not back away from whatever they were facing. Being clothed in strength and dignity does not eliminate the challenges. The challenges open doors to solutions that are only found in Christ.

Let's take a look at what God is planning while we are worried, fearful and confused concerning our future. In Jeremiah 29:11 it reads, "'For I know the plans I have for you,' says the Lord. 'They are plans for good and not for disaster, to give you a future and hope.'" Did you hear that? God knows what He is doing and no part of your life, neither past, present or future are after-thoughts. You are on the mind of God, and God desires the very best for you. There is no good thing that God will withhold from you (Psalm 84:11). Everything that is good, pleasing and perfect is what God desires to give to you and work in you. That's right, there is a work that God wants to do in your heart which will produce amazing things in your life. Strength and dignity are not attained by making all of the right choices or saying all of the right things. Strength and dignity are a part of your make-up. It's in your God-given DNA to live and walk in strength and dignity. God does not hope this for you - He declares that it is yours.

Rest in what God says about you in His Word because as long as you live, people will try to identify you by their standards. At times, there will be a temptation to bend but remain strong because there will be a way of escape presented to you in every temptation. The beginning stages of your life, which are your teen years, your 20s, or even your 30s, are to build the needed foundation to support you throughout your personal journey of discovery. Don't miss learning the valuable lessons imparted throughout God's Word and through the decisions you have and will make. Every circumstance is either a lesson learned or a lesson taught, but either way, it is a lesson.

Never allow this world to strip you of the strength and dignity that you've been designed to wear. Live your life with no fear as you rest on the promises of God concerning you.

CHAPTER 3

"The Gift Called You"

"We now have this light shining in our hearts, but we
ourselves are like fragile clay jars containing this
great treasure. This makes it clear that our great
power is from God, not from ourselves."
2 Corinthians 4:7 (NLT)

Have you ever wondered why it seems as if everyone
else is progressing, becoming more beautiful, getting the
attention from the guy you are interested in, and overall
doing what you're not? I know, I too have thought this way
plenty of times. I spent years comparing myself to what
others had or what other people were doing, but I had to
come to a place of self-reflection. I had to think of what
factors I was using to identify myself. I had to consider that
maybe I had created an unrealistic perception of who I was,
who I could become. I had to reassess the motivations that
were leading me from one point to the other. I took a long

hard look at my life and began to seek God concerning my worth and value in Him.

I must admit that this was not an easy journey. In truth, it is a journey that is far from over but a journey that we each must welcome as a necessary element of our growth. This is for both young and old. No one can convince you of your worth, and no one creates a mindset of your worth for you. It must be what you believe for yourself and what you live out daily, with or without the applause and approval of others. Understanding that you are a gift, a treasure, and a daughter of the King is the foundation upon which your worth and value will be established upon. It's not about what other people have told you, it's about the truth that comes from your Creator. Often when a person really wants to understand the value of a possession, they must go back to the creator and begin to ask questions. In this same way, to understand your value, you must seek God and learn His original purpose for your life.

According to Zechariah 2:8; we are called the "apple of God's eye." In some translations, we are called God's "most precious possession." How amazing is that?! God looks at us in spite of what we've done, despite what we've thought of ourselves and calls us a "prize," something of great worth. You see, often when we look at ourselves, we don't think that our lives contain any type of treasure, let alone be worthy of being considered precious. But the reality is, that when God created us, He knew exactly what He was doing and, He did so with perfection. The problem is not how God created us, the problem is that we are not entirely embracing who God has created us to be. We live in a culture that says you must dress a certain way, use certain words, and have a specific amount of followers on social media in order to be deemed of any importance; but this is not the truth in the Kingdom of God.

At this moment, it is my prayer that you are encouraged, uplifted and reminded that you are far more valuable than what the eye can see. That your worth and value is not defined by what you wear, how you speak, or the amount of followers that you have. You were created with a purpose. The plan that God has for your life far exceeds what you could ever imagine. The amazing thing about trusting God in this process of becoming who you really are is that when you truly surrender your thoughts to Him, transformation takes place. Maybe you have spent the majority of your life feeling as if you didn't measure up or that you didn't look "the part," but did you know that you serve a God that looks at you and calls you His daughter? That's right, you are the apple of His eye. You are indeed a treasure. People around you may not be aware that they are blessed because of who you are but don't allow that to stop you from being able to see what you have in you. You were built to last, created to stand out!

Life will not always go as we plan. However, it will certainly go just as God has planned for it to be. You were created to shine; created to shine because of the light of Jesus that lives within. Often we allow our shine to fade because of the lack of significance that we give God. We often live our lives trying to create an identity outside of God, but we shine the most as DOTK when we walk in the fulfillment of who we are in HIM. Do you realize that the more He becomes a part of your life, the more you actually begin to truly live the life that God intended you to live? There is no way you can fully live a life that is treasured without gaining your significance from your relationship with God. We often turn to other things such as friends, relationships, and worldly gain for identification, but all ground outside of God will not be as firm as we might think. At some point, we will find ourselves sinking rather than standing. We must come to a place where we realize that it is not only in our weakness that God is strong. It is when we make the decision to be vulnerable before God that we actually begin to understand His strength and our security in Him.

The gift of being you is God's way of saying, "Open your eyes and see what is before you. Don't miss what you have by focusing on what you don't have." This is indeed what often happens in our attempt to be known, seen, or acknowledged; we often lose ourselves, eventually letting go of the foundation that we once had in God. However, the key to maintaining the foundation that has been established in your relationship with God is consistency. *The moment we stop doing, saying, and living in a way that cultivates and validates who we are in Christ is the same moment that we, like jewels, begin to lose our shine.*

Have you ever seen jewelry in a display window? It seems to sparkle and shine endlessly. In the same way, that jewelry needs to be shined, polished, and cared for is the same way in which God desires for us to maintain our relationship with Him. This happens by way of personal devotional time, prayer, reading the Word, sharing with friends, and being in environments that are conducive to the growth of your walk in faith. When these things don't happen our shine (our lives) grows dim and the once vibrant and exciting outlook that we once had becomes a fleeting memory.

I know that we have a lot that happens from day to day that tries to rob us of our time, our worth, our lady-like character, and our relationship with God. Ultimately we must protect our relationship just as fine jewelry is protected. Think of how many times you've gone into a jewelry store and just asked to try on a necklace or ring that you knew was above your pay grade. Remember the facial expressions that you may have received from the sales consultant because he or she knew that you were trying on what you could not afford. Now, interestingly enough, the sales consultant was not concerned with how the item would look on you as much as they were concerned with you handling the item with care. Do you see where I am going with this? In the same way, that the salesperson is given a job to be careful with the merchandise and cautious with the people who handle their fine jewelry, is the same way in which we must watch over the treasure and gift that has been given to us by God; the gift of self.

Sure, you will have girlfriends that will need you at midnight as well as relationships that may keep you up all night from time to time. However, at the end of the day, you must be able to recognize and identify that your time, life, and efforts are all treasures to be honored, protected, and looked after. I remember as a teenager I began to realize that no one would look at my time or efforts. In fact, people would take all of the time that I would give and think nothing of it. At some point, my eyes were opened to the treasure and gift that I was and I made some changes. I began to look at the patterns of some of my friendships, I began to think of the 50/50 concept and had, to be honest with myself; even on a good day, I was giving them about seventy-five percent while I was given about twenty-five. It was not an easy adjustment, but I can tell you that ten years later I see the benefits of the decisions I made back then.

The Gift Called "You" Reminder

- Every day make it your mission to assess the ways in which you are spending your time.

- Think of the things that were done that produced very little. If you are giving your time, space, and energy to things that do not produce fruit, you will begin to feel drained and empty.

- Acknowledge the importance of "you" time. This is personal time that needs to be taken out for you and God; not time for you, God, your friend's relationship problems, etc. Taking out this time will be a "tank filler" (an act that will bring you life and encourage you in a personal way to regain focus on the things that matter the most to you).

- Ask yourself this hard question: Did I give out more than what was deposited? We rarely see that we are giving way more than what is being received and as a result, we hit rock bottom, completely depleted because we have given all that we could and took no time for the "tank fillers" in our lives.

43

- Take the time to fully embrace what you have at the moment. If we know how to do anything at all, it's planning for tomorrow. This is not in and of itself a bad thing, but when we start missing out on the blessings and gifts that are here today because of our hopes in tomorrow, we only rob ourselves.

It is my prayer that these simple reminders give you a starting point as to how you can identify the various ways in which the gift of life and the gift called "you" can be optimized. I remember hearing someone say a long time ago that if "the devil can't make you bad; he will certainly make you busy." The relevancy to this about our culture and our overall view of worth and value play a significant role in the truth found in that statement. We spend most of our time trying to find things to occupy our time or create projects that create "productivity," but all we are doing is staying busy with the wrong things. The enemy doesn't mind the time that is wasted on idle things because he knows that the more we determine our worth on what we accomplish, the easier is to lose sight of who we are in Christ. Our efforts of achievement do not define us. Our identity is in Christ. Sometimes we aren't losing out because of what we *aren't* doing; rather we are losing out because of what we *are* doing. Life can be very busy and demanding, but keep in mind that each one of us has the responsibility given to us - by God - to use wisdom and to take ownership of our time. Be careful to guard your time, guard your heart, guard your life, and defend your relationship with Christ.

According to the opening scripture of this chapter, we see that our strength comes from God. This means that even on our greatest day of strength, it is God who ultimately empowers us to do what we do. In fact, when we really think about it, what the scripture is saying is that it is the light of Christ that shines within us. Our bodies are nothing more than jars of clay. Our lives are fragile and often shattered, but with the treasure of Christ that lives within, we have new meaning. Life has new meaning. This is why we can experience so much in our bodies (sickness, heartache, pains, etc.) and still have a sense of peace and stability because of Christ. We, ourselves, are weak and in that place of weakness according to 2 Corinthians 12:9, God's strength is made perfect. We aren't weak to acknowledge that we don't have all of the answers and that we aren't sufficient without God. It is when we place God in a box and try to do everything ourselves that we are at our weakest.

Understanding your value as a DOTK is understanding that it's not weak to stand in need of God and to embrace His pursuit. It takes great strength to be willing to surrender. It doesn't matter what you've experienced or who has tried to stand in your way. All that matters is that you are on the right path with God. God desires to shine through our weakness and to shine through all those that try to shield His presence from being in our lives. Allow yourself to take full advantage of what God is offering, take Him out of the box and let His light shine through you. You are a gift that God desires to present to the world on a daily basis. You are His masterpiece (Ephesians 2:10). You are His treasure. Allow your life to be the gift that God desires to unwrap for all of the world to see, the gift called You.

Your life in Christ is the gift that the world is waiting to unwrap.

CHAPTER 4

"Precious"

"How precious are your thoughts about me, O God!
They are innumerable! I can't even count them; they
outnumber the grains of sand! And when I wake up in
the morning, you are still with me!" Psalm 139:17-18
(NLT)

When I wake up, He is still with me; that is just a sweet reminder to me that no matter what happened the day before and no matter how tough it will get today, He is still with me. Have you ever gotten your hands wet at the lake or ocean and then touched the sand and tried counting all the grains? God's thoughts regarding you cannot even be numbered, for the number would be far greater than the total amount of individual grains of sand on the planet. That's a lot of thoughts! He doesn't give up on us, He won't throw us away. God finds incredible worth in you. So, no matter how broken and no matter how messed up your life is, He still wants to be a part of your life. God can't stop thinking about YOU! You are His beautiful creation whom He loves and adores. To me, this is what being treasured means; knowing He will never leave me nor forsake me no matter what. I picked this verse because I feel it captures the aroma of the amazing and perfect love that He so graciously lavishes on us.

"God loves each of us as though there were only one of us." — St. Augustine*

Anna McIvor, Treasured Girl

What an amazing picture of God's amazing love for us. To think that we often count ourselves out and then become crippled by the lies that we believe, when all the while God can't stop thinking about us. It's interesting how we will become stuck in yesterday, like Anna mentioned, never understanding that God has forgiven us and has never walked away. Maybe you read the scripture above and thought to yourself, "There is no way God thinks of me that way," but it's true. Just look at what He says. In the midst of everything that you have experienced and in the midst of every hardship, God is with you. In fact, while you are in those hard places, God desires for you to experience His love and presence even more.

Maybe you've convinced yourself that your past is too dark, that light could never enter. You couldn't be more wrong. In fact, God has come to be the light in and through you! That's right, God desires to shine through you so that when people look at you, they see a reflection of Him. According to Matthew 5:16, we are to "let our good deeds shine out for all to see so that everyone will praise our heavenly Father." This scripture in many ways demonstrates our ability to not only represent Christ but to look like Him in our words and in our actions. There are doors that God desires to open for you, but you must first see that you are positioned for what's on the other side. Sure, there may be things that make you feel like you aren't prepared or "godly" enough. However, do you realize that God is only looking for someone that is willing? It's not about what you could do for God, it is about what you will allow God to do through you. God prepares and He positions. It's not about making yourself ready, but you being correctly positioned for God to prepare you. Are you willing to turn your back on your yesterdays and allow your today to reflect the grace, love, and favor of God that He desires to pour upon you?

There are many things that God desires to reveal to us. One of the most prevalent truths is just how important you are to Him. God wants for you to know His love, encounter His love, and allow your life to be changed by His love. Will you open your heart to the reality that God desires to give you His love? Will you no longer remain where you were and dwell on what your yesterdays have told you? How unfortunate it is, that some of us will never open the free gift of love that God has given. Even at this moment, you may be reading this thinking that you just can't do it, you just can't let go. But do you realize that you are so precious to God that He gave His only son so that you could let go? He gave His son so that you could let go of the hurt, let go of the rejection, let go of the fear, let go of what they said about you, and let go of what they did to you. God makes a life of freedom accessible to us. Let's make a decision as a daughter of the Most-High God to never allow ourselves to be bound to what was, preventing us from seeing what is.

Have you ever woken up in the morning disappointed or hurt because of a not-so-lovely decision that was made the day or night before? You may have thought to yourself when you went to sleep, that if you could just sleep it off everything would be okay. You thought to yourself that when you woke up maybe the hurt and pain that you were currently experiencing would leave. However, to your dismay, this was not the case at all. It was so far from the truth that all you wanted to do was sleep and numb yourself from what you've experienced. Remember that when David said, "And when I wake up, you are still with me," what he was saying is that in the eyes of God, yesterday does not stop His love, His presence in our lives, or His desire for us. *He is not running from us because of our yesterday, He is staying with us because of our today.*

"Precious"

For many of us, the ability to believe that there *is* someone who loves everything about us and does not turn away because of our imperfections or insecurities is usually far from our reality. However, when we have an authentic and personal encounter with God, our lives are changed, and our perspective is transformed. Maybe at this moment, this seems unrealistic and unattainable but let's take a look at a few steps that can empower us focused on our today and keep us from dwelling on our yesterday.

Walking in Your Today and Leaving Yesterday

- Remind yourself that, you are identified by what you believe, what you willingly allow to stand in the way of growth, or allow to propel you into your tomorrow. When we allow ourselves to be defeated because of our yesterday, we rob ourselves from being able to truly experience the beauty of our today. Move away from what was and allow God to move you into what is and what will be.

- Surround yourself with people that are reminding you of who you are and not who you were. One of the primary reasons why we stay stuck is because of what we allow people to speak over us. "The tongue can bring death or

51

life; those who love to talk will reap the consequences." Proverbs 18:21 (NLT)

- Think of the time that you invest in what was and how much of that time can be spent instead on what is, and how you can prepare for the future. Most of the time, we are so preoccupied with what was that we rarely learn to live in, appreciate, or celebrate what is. Don't invest your time and energy into that which has no ability to reciprocate in production.

- Keep your mind focused on what will be. As you do this, you are giving your "right now" more significance than your yesterday. Sure, your past plays a significant role in setting the foundation, but the decisions that you consistently choose are the decisions that will move you forward.

- Think of all of the lessons learned in your past and how you have been empowered by them and not set back. The thing about your past is, it's not a bad thing at all. However, when you magnify the negative experiences and minimize the positive you miss the blessing that is found in every circumstance.

- Remind yourself that Christ came to make all things new. Don't force yourself to stay in what was when Christ came so that you can experience the blessings and benefits of living a new life in Him.

It is my prayer that you give yourself the gift of unconditional love by opening your heart to what God says and thinks about you. This may not happen overnight but, it will happen with time and placing your trust in God. In the same way, that the grains of sand cannot be measured, the thoughts of God concerning you cannot be measured. The incredible factor in God's love is that it's a "one-way" type of love. God is not sitting back and saying, "Love me first and I will love you back." Rather, He did the exact opposite according to 1 John 4:10. We find in this scripture that God loved us first. His love was "one-way." God knew how He wanted to show His love and how His love for us would be used for both our good and His glory.

Think of the times when you have felt loved the most and reflect on the fact that Christ said that there is "no greater love than this than a man would lay down his life for a friend." Think of how many people that you have in your life right now that would die for you. How many did you come up with? Well, if you are anything like me, you were able to name maybe a very close family member but other than that, your list is probably limited. Not only does this show the unconditional love of God, but it also shows man's conditional love. No one can love you like God, not even on their best day. So, while you are trying to convince yourself that you are not worthy or good enough for this kind of love, think of how God's love has been with you from day one.

We are so precious to God that He even has our names written on the palm of His hand according to Isaiah 49:16. What an image! We have a hard time thinking that God thinks of us during our struggles, when according to Isaiah and also the opening scripture, we see not only God thinking of us, but God thinking of us all of the time, with joy. Our lives are testaments of God's faithfulness and His commitment to us. God is indeed committed to the promises He has declared over our lives. He is faithful and shall bring to pass what He has declared. Our inability to see what God has said before God does it is often a challenge. However, when you know who you are in Him, life begins to look a lot different.

Now, I understand for some of you who have never heard your father say that you were beautiful or that you have a bright future ahead, what you read throughout scripture may be a challenge. Some of you may not have met your father, but allow me to tell you firsthand (I personally did not have a relationship with my birth father growing up) that God is able to do for you what no other man can. God is able to literally comfort you in the middle of a crisis and rock you in His arms. I recall many nights crying myself to sleep, I felt God holding me and telling me that everything would be okay. I remember those nights like they were yesterday, only because some of them were not too long ago. You see, when we as DOTK take our rightful place with the Father we begin to fully receive His love, not because it was limited before, but because we had not fully embraced the depth of what God had given. Look at what David says here concerning God's view of us:

> *"What are mere mortals that you should think about them, human beings that you should care for them? Yet you made them only a little lower than God and crowned them with glory and honor. You gave them charge of everything you made, putting all things under their authority – the flocks and the herds and all the wild animals, the birds in the sky, the fish in the sea, and everything that swims in the ocean."*
> Psalm 8:4-8

I don't know about you, but I wouldn't put someone in charge over something that I've created unless I truly valued them, trusted them, and had great confidence in their abilities. I would look not only at what the person says but their heart as well. This is what God does with us. He knows that we sometimes feel in our heart what we are not saying with words and in those moments, God searches our heart. For most of us, when He searches our heart He sees the young girl that feels abandoned, lonely, misunderstood, and often forgotten. He looks at where we are today, and He considers what we have left behind, what we've held on to, and He says to us, at this moment, *"No matter what was lost, no matter what was gained, I love you and see far more value in you than what you could ever imagine. In fact, when I look at you, I see the precious gem that you are. You may have been broken once before, you may even be broken right now, but if you allow me to, I can mend all brokenness, and I can do in you what no one else can."*

You are a daughter of the King, and there is no hurt that God cannot heal. He desires to take away every moment that keeps us from seeing the crown that He has placed on our heads. We are daughters of the Most-High and that means that we are a big deal to God. We have been called for His purpose and to reflect His light and love to others. May I encourage you at this moment to walk with confidence knowing who you are and who your God is? Walk in confidence knowing who you are in Him. You may not have confidence in your abilities because of the limitations that you have created, but have faith in God. Proverbs 3:25-26 says, "Do not be afraid of sudden terror, nor of trouble from the wicked when it comes; for the Lord will be your confidence, and will keep your foot from being caught" (NKJV). God desires to protect and shield us. It's His desire that we rest in His abilities and are constantly reminded that it's in Him that we are able to do all things (Acts 17:28).

As you reflect on the words and declarations written in this chapter, I encourage you to think of the ways in which you have minimized the value God had placed upon you and things that have kept you from seeing how precious you are in the eyes of God. As we continue to journey together, discovering the *truth about our worth and value*, let's make it our priority to let go of the things that have stood in our way. We are better than what we were yesterday and tomorrow we would be better than what we are today. Let's not let what has no relevance today stand in the way of what God will do in and through us tomorrow. We are DOTK and nothing can separate us from God's love.

> *"And I am convinced that nothing can ever separate us from God's love. Neither death nor life, neither angels nor demons, neither our fears for today nor our worries about tomorrow—not even the powers of hell can separate us from God's love. No power in the sky above or in the earth below—indeed, nothing in all creation will ever be able to separate us from the love of God that is revealed in Christ Jesus our Lord." Romans 8:38-39*

Day by day God shows His love and day by day we must have hearts that are open to this love that not only heals but frees. Our freedom is based on our willingness to let go of everything and everyone that stands in the way of what God is doing. Just as Anna encouraged us to do at the opening of this chapter, let's capture the aroma of God's amazing and perfect love that He graciously lavishes on us.

Our worth and value are defined by the Creator of every good and perfect gift. Have "faith eyes" that are able to see the gift that lies before you.

CHAPTER 5

"Flawless"

"You are altogether beautiful, my darling;
there is no flaw in you." Song of Songs 4:7(NIV)

I picked this verse because I believe that every girl should know how perfect they are. Every girl finds a flaw in themselves or in others, but we are perfect in God's eyes. Society is so messed up these days, they just point out your flaws and say that you aren't good enough, but don't let people change you. You don't need to change who you are to be flawless in others' eyes. You are already perfect in the eyes of the Creator. Don't forget that.

Kristy Houston –McMillan, Treasured Girl

Most of us spend our entire lives trying to change, eliminate, or ignore every imperfection that we see. We categorize the type of day we are having based on how we look and very rarely on what has happened throughout the day. In many ways, it seems that the more compliments we receive, the less confident we feel. It's almost as if we feel people are extending compliments to make up for the imperfections that we believe everyone notices. However, when God looks at us, He sees us as His prized possession! We are His masterpiece, and He loves us unconditionally. Look at what Solomon says concerning the beauty seen admired in a woman. We are classified as being "altogether beautiful." This means that we are beautiful as a whole being, even with the flaws we believe to have.

Kristy states that though society points out flaws and error, God doesn't. In fact, in His eyes, we have been perfectly and wonderfully made according to Psalm 139:14. Throughout this chapter allow me to challenge your perspective and help you see that you are indeed flawless. Beginning this process we must be aware of the things, and maybe even the people, that play a role in speaking life into our imperfections instead of life into our true beauty. Have you ever been around a group of girls who couldn't help but talk about either their flaws or the imperfections that they see in others? Sometimes even their own friends'? There is usually an undertone of jealousy that runs in this circle, and usually, a good number of them feel uncomfortable but do not want to say a word. Why does this happen? Could it be that we find validation in acknowledging the flaws in other people in some unhealthy way? Could it be that beneath the surface of criticism lies insecurity?

I believe that we know that there is something greater waiting for us to discover in the depths of our heart. We are aware that there is something greater, but a voice from within keeps telling us that "the greater" is reserved for everyone else but ourselves. What is it that stops us from being able to wear the crown of royalty that belongs to us? What prevents us from taking the next step to move forward in the victories that belong to us? Maybe you'd say it is friends, society, or maybe even what you see in other people, but whatever your response may be, in the midst of it all you must come to a place where you can see "the greater" for yourself.

Can you imagine the impact that is possible and the influence that is given when we stand in our rightful place as a DOTK? When we stand in that place with the King, people begin to see that our worth and value is measured by other means. Ways that cannot be understood by this world because our value is not of this world, but of God's Kingdom. When we attempt to fit in, we are trading in our privileges as Daughters of the King to minimize our infinite worth as royalty. There is nothing that this world has to offer in comparison to what God gives daily. *Though what the world is offering may seem like it has the ability to mold and shape you into perfection, what it really does is camouflage the real you and place your authenticity in a box.*

I remember reading two different articles about two beautiful Hollywood actresses. As I read these articles, I was amazed. When I looked at them, I saw perfection. I saw the "look" that most women would die for, and I saw the kind of fame that most people will never reach. However, to my surprise, these women suffered from low self-esteem, abusive relationships, and infidelity within their marriages. Both women explained in the articles that they felt like they had no value outside of the way they looked, so they went from relationship to relationship trying to fill that empty space in their lives. In fact, they both said that they were looking for love and hoping that people would see more than their outward beauty.

As I read the articles, I couldn't believe what I was reading. Here you have two beautiful women, one of which had been voted as being one of the most beautiful women in the world, the other has such natural beauty that you would think that she is twenty years younger than her actual age. I realized at that moment that it doesn't matter how you look, how you dress, or the money that you make; all that matters is that you should find your significance in a source/foundation that never waivers. I would imagine that the fame of these women had placed them in a league of their own, but it was a league that left them lonely and desperately searching for truth and meaning. No matter how flawless these women appeared to be; beneath the surface, they were broken, and their image was left shattered in pieces.

How ironic is that; the people who seem to have it all, most of the time, have nothing and the people we often overlook as being "unimportant," are the ones who understand that their significance does not come from anyone or anything but God Himself? I am challenged as I write this book because there are indeed moments where I often think less of myself because of the beauty that I admire in another. But you know what? In those moments, God - in a way that only He can - reels me in and reminds me of His word in Psalm 139 and Song of Songs 4. No matter how alone you may feel when lies enter your mind, you aren't alone.

The reality is not what you have experienced, what you have thought of yourself, or what other people have said. The reality is what you do after the experiences, after the thoughts, and after the words that have been said. We will spend our lives either embracing the beauty that lives within us, or we will spend our lives rejecting that beauty. The choice is not left to anyone else, but ourselves. It's a decision that we must come to and a decision that will carry us through the low moments that are experienced.

It is my desire to "...lead a life that is worthy of the calling" (Ephesians 4:1).It is also my hope and prayer that you, my sister, are able to do the same! We are so precious in God's sight, and we were made perfect in His image. *We don't lack because of what we don't have; we are living in lack because of what we choose to believe.* There is nothing that can separate us from God's love, just like there is nothing that can separate us from walking in the manifestation of all that God desires to give. The question is, will we as DOTK allow the love of the Father to mend the broken and shattered images of ourselves that we've believed? The amazing part of knowing who we are through whose we are is knowing who we *aren't* and how we no longer have to identify ourselves. When we begin to accurately identify ourselves through Jesus Christ, there is little to no room at all to believe anything outside of the absolute truth.

The truth of who we are is established in knowing who we are not, but unfortunately, we spend so much time speaking life into who we aren't that it becomes a great challenge to identify with who we are. I remember having the opportunity to hear a group of young ladies share their testimony of life in prostitution. They started out very young, and before they knew it, their lives had become entangled by the trap of the enemy. Even in moments when they wanted "out" they couldn't see past what they had done, and who they had become. But one day, God grabbed a hold of them, led them to the Word of God (their truth) and showed them how they are new when they accepted Him. They began to read about how God desired to remove all of their sins and give them a new start (Ephesians 2:10). It wasn't until they realized that God wanted to give them a new start and that they were never created to live the life that they were living, that they began to see the truth.

It's not until we truly open our hearts to the truth of God's Word concerning who we are, turn a deaf ear to the lies that have tormented and falsely classified us as something that we aren't, that we truly begin to see the truth of who we are in God. Maybe your story is not like theirs. Maybe your struggle was not prostitution, but compromise concerning boundaries, or lying to get your way. Whatever your story may be, the destination that God has created for us is all the same, and that is "New Life in Him". According to 2 Corinthians 5:17 it says, "This means that anyone who belongs to Christ has become a new person. The old life is gone; a new life has begun!" What victory we have because of Christ! What a blessing and joy it is to know that the old life has been done away with and that there is new life in Christ!

Our lives have the ability to produce good fruit no matter how bad the tree once was. Our lives can be made whole in Christ, and our perception of self can be renewed through Him. We were created flawlessly in the image of God and yet marred in the eyes of man. However, the blessing in it all is that, once God places His stamp of approval on us, nothing that man does or says can take it away.

Let who you are in Christ speak louder than who you aren't to the world.

CHAPTER 6

"The Trap of Comparison"

"In his grace, God has given us different gifts for doing certain things well..." Romans 12:6 (NLT)

Have you ever met someone that seemingly did everything with perfection? It didn't matter if it was singing, a job, dressing, a degree or house; it just seemed like when you were around them, you came up short on nearly everything. As much as you liked them as a friend, you couldn't help but compare yourself to them on many occasions. You couldn't put your finger on it, but there was something about them that drew you to remain friends. It didn't take long before you began thinking that you would never measure up to her that you began to distance yourself. Not only distancing yourself from her but others that brought about some form of competition as well. If only you had read this book sooner, you would have been able to apply the "Compliment, Don't Compare (CDC)" tips.

Compliment, Don't Compare (CDC)

- Compliment your sister (friend) on things that are done well that may be a weak area for you.

- Compliment your sister when she is wearing something that only she could pull off.

- Compliment your sister when she takes advice from you and the situation turns out great.

- Compliment your sister when you feel like there are things that you have learned from her.

One of the most challenging things to do is to compliment someone in something that we wish we could do but is not our gift. According to Romans 12, we have all been given gifts and abilities and all of which vary from person to person. No matter what it looks like no single person is perfect (amazing at everything). We all have our shortcomings or weak areas, and they are to be embraced just as much as our strengths. When you are able to give compliments even though you feel like comparing, you create a foundation for understanding the full value in your friendships. I remember looking at one friend in particular and literally wanting to be them. I wanted to look like them and at one point I even wanted their family. In my mind, they had a perfect life. That is until they informed me otherwise.

The trap of comparison is a tool that the enemy uses to rob us of our worth and value. It is a tool that works for most of us. We spend our lives holding compliments hostage, hosting envy in our hearts, and comparing our lives to the lives of others around us. But take a look at the scriptures that we have been reading. God thinks highly of each and every one of us, and He has made all of us different, giving each of us our own gifts and abilities. According to Psalm 139:14, we have been made wonderfully complex! Do you know what that means? It means that no one person is the same. We are all different, and these differences should be celebrated because that's what makes us wonderfully complex and absolutely unique.

What would the world be like if we were all the same? Boring. There would be no character or pizzazz to life because we would be clones of one another. God created complexities/differences in His amazing plan (us) so that we could celebrate, enjoy, and learn from each other. Everything that someone else does doesn't mean that we must learn to do it too at some point. Sometimes, the gifts that we see in someone else are being made visible to simply be admired and appreciated. It can be hard to see or admire something in someone that we want for ourselves, but in those situations, I think it's always a great practice to first know what's in *your* heart and then ask questions concerning their personal journey.

Recently, I stepped out of my comfort zone and reached out to a couple through social media that I admire. They are a power couple for sure and are doing amazing things to build God's Kingdom. I prayed about it and then I felt God gave me the nodding approval to reach out and ask questions. Not only was I blown away by their sincerity but also thankful for their immediate response. I can't begin to tell you how one message changed everything for me concerning the publication of my books and various contacts throughout the process. It's amazing what God will do when our hearts are in the right place. *When we learn that the strengths of others can be a strength to us, we stop viewing the strengths of others as a magnification of our weaknesses.* It is true that there are highly gifted and talented people in this world, even what society would deem as geniuses. However, what is considered a compliment for another cannot be viewed as a ridicule for yourself.

I love how God can change our thinking by simply showing us what lies within. If we are honest, we compared ourselves to others because they have something or are doing something that we desire for ourselves. We don't know how they did it, and sometimes we automatically feel like their success is because they are "one of those lucky ones," whatever that means. But the truth is, when we seek God, more than we're looking for the attainment of others, success is sure to come. Success does not come because we have chased it down, but because we pursued God; the one who leads us into success and provisions. Joshua 1:7-8 reads:

> *"Be strong and very courageous. Be careful to obey all the instructions Moses gave you. Do not deviate from them, turning either to the right or to the left. Then you will be successful in everything you do. Study this Book of Instruction continually. Meditate on it day and night so you will be sure to obey everything written in it. Only then will you prosper and succeed in all you do."*

Success is not found in our pursuit of it, it is found in our pursuit of Him. There is no need to compare what you have or don't have to someone else. God holds your life in the palm of His hand and your success is a result of your pursuit of Him. There are various passages throughout the Bible, such as 1 Corinthians 12:21, 1 Peter 4:10, and Ephesians 4:11 that give emphasis on the value and worth of all people and how we are all needed for God's purpose. We are all needed for God's work and all of our gifts are valid. God has created us equal and despite the feelings that may come, we are all viewed the same way in God's eyes.

The Trap of Comparison

- The Trap of Comparison will have you second guessing your worth and value all because of what you admire about another.

- The Trap of Comparison will have you losing sight of your skills and abilities because you are focused on someone else's.

- The Trap of Comparison will have you missing the plan that God has for your life because you desire the life of another.

- The Trap of Comparison will have you losing sight of the value in your friendships because of jealousy.

- The Trap of Comparison will always leave you feeling as if you aren't good enough.

- The Trap of Comparison will stop you from moving forward.

Don't allow the Trap of Comparison to lead you away from the plan of God and onto the path of someone else. You are beautiful, called, and destined for great things and what God has for you is indeed for you. There is nothing that can snatch away the blessings or talents that God has given you.

"The Trap of Comparison"

Admiring the gifts of another should be something that points you back to a position of praise to God. Every good and perfect gift comes from Him! When God looks at your life, He declares it to be a "Good Gift."

Don't rob others of the blessings that would come along when you are walking in the plan and purpose that you have been created for! You are a blessing just as you are and the gifts that God had given you work best when you acknowledge their value. When we minimize what God is doing in us because of the "grand" things that we think He is doing with other people, we miss it. My sister this is the plan of the enemy—for us to be blind and miss what God is doing. The plan of the enemy is for us to lose sight of what God has said, what God is doing, and the ways in which God works. He comes to steal, kill, and to destroy (John 10:10). One of the ways that He does that is by using the open doors of vulnerability that we have not entirely given over to God.

We must be willing, as Daughters of the King, to be honest concerning our insecurities and lies that have entered into our minds. When we do this, we are submitting those things to God, which takes any ability away from the enemy to use against us. If you begin to feel low in those moments of comparison, it's important to give those things to God. Even in the more common ways in which this happens through social media, it is equally as important. Nowadays we see the highlight reel of the lives of many people from day to day and, if we aren't careful, we will confuse social media life for reality. Most people won't share the things that have hurt them or the ways in which they've hurt themselves as an attempt to fit in, but it is there. The pain lives in the same place that we often see smiles and happy status updates. It's on social media - artificial friendships and synthetic personalities, so keep in mind that what you see is not always what you get.

Take an extra measure today to declare the following words over your life and ask God to fill the areas of your life where the Trap of Comparison has caused hurt .

> I declare that I am a daughter of the King and that my gifts and abilities have been given to me to be a blessing to people around me. I declare that I will not allow what I see in others to stop me from seeing what God is doing in me. I take every thought captive to the obedience of Christ at this moment and I declare that I do have a purpose, and my life makes a difference. God, I ask you to remove the fear and the mask that I often wear in those moments when it becomes hard for me to be authentic. More than anything, I desire to be a reflection of you, and I know that you make no mistakes. I declare that I am treasured, I am valued, and my friendships are a reflection of God's love and desire for unity. I will not walk in fear, and I will not compare my life to anyone else because I know that

my life has been signed, sealed, and delivered with my name on it.

When you feel down and out, remind yourself of who you are in God. Remind yourself that you are who you are, because of who God is in you. There is no competition in the Kingdom of God, for we are all needed. Allow your friendships to flourish and let your admiration for those around you to give you joy, knowing that you are connected with people who are walking in the fulfillment of their calling. Continue to move forward and allow nothing to hold you back. God has not brought you to where you are today for you to give up because you see something "better" or because someone does something with ease that is a challenge for you. *Learn how to ask the right questions when you admire the journey of those around you. You never know how your life and your process can be blessed by simply reaching out.*

The next time you are with friends, and they are looking "fly" or have a fabulous new hair color, compliment and do not compare. You don't even have to say, "I should do something different with my hair" because you are working on complimenting and not comparing at this point. When we feel like we need to change something about ourselves because of how appealing it looks on someone else, *sometimes* the root is comparison. I am not saying that you can't, nor should you, want something because of how it looks on a friend. What I am saying is, to make sure that your desire is out of admiration and not envy, comparison, or competition.

This chapter may be one of the more challenging chapters of the book, but it is my prayer that you are inspired to be 100% authentically you. You have so much to offer just as you are, so before wanting more of something, be sure that you have lived an entirely minimalistic life, pouring out your resources, tools, and gifts so that others may be blessed. You don't have to spend another day living vicariously through the life of another. Take note of what God is doing, make a decision to do more today than what you did yesterday, with what you have right now, and shine like the diamond you have been created to be.

Life is full of unexpected moments, blessings that were not asked for, and opportunities that were long forgotten. But when you rest in God and in His strength, you open your life up to endless possibilities and a life that is without limits. Trust God to remove the walls that insecurity has built and the limitations that had been created in comparison. Dare to believe for God to do things in you that have never been done before and make a commitment to do something for God that you've never done before. You are needed, your gifts are needed, and living life in the lane that has been mapped out for you is necessary as well.

Switching lanes and often passing people up can be tempting, but when you are walking in the plan that God has for you, you quickly realize that you are in a lane of your own and, no matter the speed, you will remain in God's perfect will and in His perfect timing. Remember that you are not identified by others or by what you accomplish. You are identified by the characteristics that have been given to you by God. Nothing can diminish your worth and value. God called you from the very beginning. According to Jeremiah 1:5, God says, "I knew you before I formed you in your mother's womb. Before you were born, I set you apart and appointed you as my prophet to the nations." How refreshing and liberating it is to know that before we were born, God had already destined our lives for greatness. It had nothing to do with what we thought but what He had placed inside us.

Measure your worth and value not by what you can do, but by what God can do through you.

(When we take the pressure off of ourselves to perform, we then see that it's God's show and that He alone is the one who takes center stage.)

CHAPTER 7

Let Go and Let Love Flow

Instead, be kind to each other, tenderhearted,
forgiving one another, just as God through Christ has
forgiven you." Ephesians 4:32 (NLT)

I chose this verse because forgiving others is difficult to do, especially when you or your loved ones have been hurt. It's challenging to be kind to those who've caused hurt and pain, especially when it's not in your heart to do so. I think that it's important for us to hear this because there will be hurt in all of our lives. However, we are to forgive others just as our Father has forgiven us. God forgives us daily, so for us to hold on to unforgiveness in our hearts is against the plan of God. God forgives us because He wants to and loves us unconditionally.

Madison Schultz, Treasured Girl

We all share hurts and pains in our lives, but what some of us do not share is our willingness to forgive.

Though we have been recipients of God's amazing grace and favor, forgiveness is something we often are challenged in extending to others. I remember someone came to me recently and asked, "How did you forgive your parents for not being there for you during your childhood years?" I remember my response being a reminder of all the times that I've stood in need of forgiveness and the fact that I have never experienced a back turned to me. You see, when I fully began to understand how much God loved me and who (Jesus) He gave up for me, it gave me a new perspective on forgiveness.

I believe that when we realize how undeserving we are of all the things God does for us and all of the times that He has forgiven us, our hearts are softened. I know we don't like to consider the fact that we have hardened hearts towards those who have brought hurt, but it's the truth. This is why it's so important to give your pain and burdens to God. He is the only one who can lift the load and remove the residue of what we have experienced. *It is one thing to say that we have forgiven, but it's another to say that we have let go.* It is in the moment of letting go that God's love can truly flow. However, when we are still holding a grudge against those who have hurt us, in many ways what we are doing is clogging the pipeline of love.

May I encourage you to consider your role as a Daughter of the King and what that truly means about how we love others? We are called to be a walking billboard of God's love. As we become more like Christ, our love grows to become more perfect. Look at what the apostle John says in his first letter:

> *"All who confess that Jesus is the Son of God have God living in them, and they live in God. We know how much God loves us, and we have put our trust in his love. God is love, and all who live in love live in God, and God lives in them. And as we live in God, our love grows more perfect. So we will not be afraid on the day of judgment, but we can face him with confidence because we live like Jesus here in this world. Such love has no fear because perfect love expels all fear. If we are afraid, it is for fear of punishment, and this shows that we have not fully experienced his perfect love. We love each other because he loved us first."(1 John 4:15-19 NLT)*

Our ability to love others grows more perfect as we live in God. The amazing thing about this text is that, when you read it thoroughly and allow it to sit with you for a moment, you are able to see a number of things. The first factor in loving people that we can take from the text is that our declaration that Jesus is the Son of God demonstrates God living in us. This confession is giving us the ability to do what we are naturally incapable of doing on our own. It is giving us capacity to love, not our own way, but His. The second factor is that as we live in God, we are living in love. This not only breaks down how we love people but it also breaks down our love through Christ. The third factor in loving people based on this scripture is that our love will not grow unless we are living in God. Allow me to take a moment and encourage you, my sister, because we cannot be sure that we are living in love if we aren't able to identify what living in God looks like.

The simplest way to define what "living in God" means is by calling it surrender. When we surrender our lives daily to the will of God, we are living in God. But, when we take matters into our own hands, we have removed God from the driver's seat of our lives and have replaced Him with ourselves. There is no way we can live in God's love when we are not living God's way. Our daily surrender to the will of God and our daily obedience to Him is not only our worship to God, but it is also our love for God. So now that we have an understanding of what "living in God" means, we can assess if we are doing just that.

The fourth factor that we can take away from living in God and loving others is that when we do this with our whole heart, there is no fear. Fear has been removed because we have fully embraced the love of God and have also fully embraced our ability to love others God's way. In reference to loving others, we must understand that this love is not because we feel like it; not because we feel obligated to do so out of guilt. The kind of love that God desires for us to bestow upon one another is love that is not conditioned to a circumstance or situation. God is able to remove the hurt that has enabled you from loving and give you the strength to let it go and to allow His love to flow through you. It's not anything you can give on your own; it is only given out to a surrendered heart.

There will be people who will come and go just as Kristy said. These people who come into your life will not always leave having been a blessing to you. However, when you are able to move past the hurt and embrace the love of God, then and only then does true forgiveness come forth. I remember being told and often telling others that, "Forgiving people does not make what was done okay. Forgiving brings personal freedom from the anger and often the bitterness that accompanies challenging situations." Maybe you have been told your entire life to "forgive and forget" but in actuality, the only way that can truly be done is through the power of the Holy Spirit. It's not possible to forget hurt and pain without receiving healing from God. Learning to let go is only found in the healing that comes from God, who takes the broken pieces of our hearts and mends them back together. God helps us to extend grace to those who have caused hurt and pain.

I love how Jesus Himself said that we (His followers, His sons, and daughters) would be known by how we love others. He didn't say that we will be recognized for how well we quoted scriptures, how often we attended church, the fact that we served in our local church, or even went on mission trips. He simply says that it's by our love. There is something so profound, yet so simple in those words because loving "despite and in spite of" can be a great struggle when there has been an offense. But God is so amazing that when we move past what happened and take a look at where we are "in spite of," a work takes place in our hearts.

Maybe you have had friends that have gossiped about you, those that you were interested in who talked about you, or even betrayed you. Perhaps you have spent a lot of your life wondering if anyone could love you just as you are. There is indeed a God, who runs the entire world who loves you just the way you are. It's true that most of us will go through a season of feeling like nothing and what we are doing isn't good enough and we, in many ways, end up treating the people who are in our lives the same. This is the truth that we rarely want to confront, let alone acknowledge that it exists. But when you allow God to walk with you down the road where the gossip and betrayal took place, you are revealing your scars, allowing God to bring healing.

The Bible says according to Colossians 3:13, we are to "Make allowance for each other's faults and forgive anyone who offends you. Remember, the Lord forgave you, so you must forgive others" (NLT). If there is any scripture that keeps me humble when it comes to forgiving others, it is this one. How quick would you be able to forgive others if you actually looked at it according to the Word? What if God only forgave you to the extent by which you forgave others? Would you then let things go instead of keeping it all inside? I know I would. When I read this scripture, I see God presenting a way of escape from offense by being the first to forgive, even in the moments where we don't acknowledge that we have done wrong. This is the amazing picture of love that God paints for us and the same picture that God desires for us to paint for others.

Romans 12:9-13 says,

"Don't just pretend to love others. Really love them. Hate what is wrong. Hold tightly to what is good. Love each other with genuine affection, and take delight in honoring each other. Never be lazy, but work hard and serve the Lord enthusiastically. Rejoice in our confident hope. Be patient in trouble, and keep on praying. When God's people are in need, be ready to help them. Always be eager to practice hospitality."

What Paul is saying to the Romans is, "Don't be fake." In other words, don't call someone your best friend today and talk about them tomorrow. View people in the light of who God has created; His workmanship, His masterpieces. Let's get on board with a policy that says, "Word of Life Only," meaning that we pledge to come aboard, committed to speaking only words that demonstrate life, not defeat or death. When our hearts are in alignment to God's way, our words will come into alignment as well. You can always tell when you haven't fully forgiven because when you see her, him, or them you instantly feel sick as if it were happening all over again.

I remember those days. I remember having such a hard time forgiving a friend of mine that I listened to a worship song that I played on repeat over and over. The words were, "I want a heart that forgives." I remember it just like it was yesterday. I remember the feelings of rage and anger rising in me and having to literally speak out loud and declare that more than anything I wanted a heart that forgives and a heart that is not easily offended. There is no reason to stay bound in your yesterday when God is trying to reveal to you an amazing tomorrow. We are more often bound by what was instead of being free to experience what will be. When we ask God to forgive us and when He does, even to the point forgetting what was done, we should feel conviction in our hearts. I know that you trusted them, and they let you down, but just as Christ forgives us we too must forgive others. Where would we be if God picked and chose when

He would forgive us and extend grace? Can you imagine what life would be like; can you imagine if God were like us? There would be very little love in the world because we often hold love hostage until something happens according to our expectations.

Can we take a minute and just thank God that He loves us relentlessly and holds nothing back from us? "Thank you for loving us with a selfless love and for extending grace when our words and actions were not in agreement with your Word. Thank you for extending a one-way kind of love that reached out to us and never let us go. Even in the moments where we wanted to let go, you held on to us. Though words do not accurately convey our gratitude at this moment for all that you've done, thank for being our father, friend, and everything else that we could ever need. Amen."

Many things play a role in being able to let go and let God's love flow. What's truly important is not found in what is holding you back. It is in understanding *how* to let go.

Letting Go:

1. To let go, you must first turn away from that which is holding you back.

2. You must remember that letting go is a state of mind just as much as it is a state if being. If you have not made it up in your mind to truly let go, your state of being will reflect that.

3. Letting go is having the ability to see more for yourself. Holding on to hurt and pain will keep you in the wrong state of mind. You must believe that you are worth more than what you experience.

4. Remember that letting go is a daily decision.

5. Letting go requires less of you and more of God. You can't hold on to the old you and your way of doing things while trying to give God permission to have full control in your life.

6. Letting go will not be easy, but you must remember that it is always worth it.

7. When you let go, you are exchanging what you had for what God desires to give.

8. To let go, you must believe that what you are about to receive is greater than what you are about to give up.

Letting go is challenging for most of us who like things done our way, at our speed, and when it's convenient. However, when you place your trust in God, you are giving up your way and daily living to live according to His. The truth is, as long as you live in the shadows of what was, the image that you see will always be in the rear view. Understand, my sister, you were born to last. You were not born to give up, back down, or bend. You were born, created, and destined to last. Stand up, dust off your shoulders and walk in your today, leaving behind your yesterday.

The beauty of life is knowing what season you are in. Know when to let go and let God's love flow.

CHAPTER 8

Forever with You

"The Lord is close to the brokenhearted and saves those who are crushed in spirit." Psalm 34:18 (NIV)

I've felt brokenhearted and crushed a lot throughout my life. Since I've gotten better from mental illness, God constantly reminds me of this verse (Hebrews 13:5), saying "I will never leave you," especially when I'm struggling. But you don't have to have a mental illness to feel broken or crushed. Sometimes it just lasts a little while, and sometimes it does turn into an illness like depression. God desires for us to be reliant on Him, to help us get through whatever it is we're going through. I believe that God wants this, because if we try to handle it our way, we'll drift and sometimes even have serious consequences. God can do anything. He can heal you from every physical and emotional scar no matter how bad it is. This verse basically just clarifies how much God wants to help and heal us. He is always near us and won't ever leave us no matter what we do. God wants to be our best friend, and He can help us get through anything. Jesus died so that we could be set free, I think if anyone is worthy to be our best friend it's Him. Trust Him. He knows what He's doing.

Kathy Davis, (KD), Treasured Girl

Haven't we all felt like we were alone, shattered, broken, and misunderstood? I know that I have. I remember feeling like KD and needing to remind myself that God's desire is for me to be completely reliant on Him! Isn't it interesting how God will use whatever our circumstance may be as a point to draw us back to Him? It doesn't matter whether we are experiencing depression, suicidal thoughts, jealousy, or rage. God can use whatever we are going through and whatever we may be feeling to draw us closer to Him. Sure, there will be days when you feel brokenhearted and just as KD says, crushed. However, we must keep in mind that in those times, don't turn away from God but to turn toward Him.

Maybe you've felt disappointed in decisions that have been made in your relationships. Maybe boundaries were crossed or even forced. Perhaps you've felt used and unappreciated. Allow me to encourage you at this moment. No matter what you've done, experienced, or thought; God declares that He will not leave you. God loves you, and He desires to blow you away with His love and compassion. KD shares her struggle with depression and mental illness and how God was the one who got her through it. However, we must first be willing to come to a place where we fully trust God and are willing to reveal our scars and hurts before Him. He is not moved by our scars and the wounds that are often left behind as a result of adverse situations. Those things bring forth compassion and love. We can either spend our lives in brokenness, or we can spend our lives walking in healing.

It's our mindset that will keep us from what is good and keep us in what is bad. It's not what has happened to us that serves as a disadvantage, it's how we respond to what has happened to us that serves as a disadvantage. At some point, we must face our past with confidence because we see our future. We have to remember that what we've experienced has only the significance that we assign to it. Our past can only create and hinder us based on what we allow. That's right! The decision is placed in our hands, and the outcome is put in God's. I know you have thought to yourself that, if God is such a loving God, then why all of the hurt and pain? But, the question that should actually be asked is, "Why all of the blessings when we are so undeserving?" You see, it's easy for us to blame God when we have our hearts broken because of a relationship, family divorce, or hardship. When do we find the time to give God what is due to Him concerning all of the amazing things that are happening?

Our brokenness is an opportunity for God to reveal Himself strong and mighty in our lives and when we allow Him to do that, healing takes place. May I encourage you, my sister, to allow God to bring the healing to your broken heart? God promises in Hebrews 13:5 that He will never leave us. This means that no matter how deep or low we may feel, God will come and rescue us. Our experiences do not stop God from healing our hearts, but our anger and unforgiveness do. I can honestly say that there have been times where I have personally experienced brokenness and didn't know what to do. I had given my all, tried my best, and remained honest, but in life, what we do has very little effect on the decisions that others make.

It's likely that your heart has been broken due to a relationship as a young girl or woman. However, it is also likely that after feeling broken and shattered you've tried to handle what you felt your own way. Trust me when I say I know what it's like. I also know the incredible restoration and peace that comes with lying that kind of weight and burden at the feet of Jesus. Sure, you can try to heal your hurt by masking it, but deep down inside the hurt remains. Our hearts are fragile. When we have placed our hearts in the hands of people who have not been prepared by God, we are bound to be hurt. Not only that, we are bound to hurt others. I don't believe we set out to hurt each other. At some point, our selfish desires get in the way of being able to see the truth of God because of our decisions. The fact is "hurt people hurt people," meaning when complete healing (not momentary appeasement) has not taken place in our lives, we become unable to love each other God's way, leaving room for error, selfish gain, and personal gratification.

You see, God promising to never leave us and to be with us in our brokenness is so that we will lean on His strength, His wisdom, and His love more than we do on our own. Despite how passionately we desire to do things God's way, without completely depending on God this becomes impossible. There is no way that we can fully embrace healing, acknowledge brokenness, or welcome God's miraculous healing without completely and relentlessly welcoming God. God is the healer. He is the mender of our broken hearts, and He is an ever present help in time of need. There are neither reasons nor excuses that we could use that make our self-reliance acceptable or profitable. At the end of the day, only what we give to God and completely let go of will cease to have power over us. But what we refuse to let go of and carry along with each new day is ultimately what weighs us down.

Have you ever thought that you were completely over what happened or that you had let go of someone that had hurt you, but in an instant, all of the feelings, emotions, pain, and memories began to flood your mind without your control? Certainly. You may have even found yourself in a state of shock by the vivid memories that arose so quickly. Do you know what's most startling about this scenario? It's that this whole time you had no clue that those feelings and emotions were still there. This not only helps us see how easy it is for us to have undealt with situations lying dormant in our hearts, but also in many ways we can very well be fooling ourselves when it comes to the truth.

Unveiling the Truth about Brokenness

- We will remain broken until we come to the realization that we cannot fix ourselves without God.

- Our brokenness will stay for as long as we allow unforgiveness to remain in our hearts.

- Brokenness is not always a reflection of what someone else has done, sometimes it's a reflection of what we have allowed. We can't spend our whole lives blaming someone else for what we've allowed.

- Brokenness is not a permanent state of being. We stay in this state by choice.

- We can receive freedom, and it doesn't have to take years. Often we are told that it takes time for our hearts to be healed once brokenness has taken place, but based on Biblical accounts of God bringing forth healing in an instant, this not true. Our healing relies on our willingness to move forward and let go.

- Brokenness is only a negative thing when we choose to remain in it.

- God will use our brokenness to reveal to us His love, compassion, and grace.

- Being broken does not mean that you are forgotten or can't be "used" again (by God).

- Our ability to see beyond today is our ability to see beyond the hurt.

The truth about how we feel and what we've experienced is often driven by emotion and very seldom our reality. So, we must be careful to not confuse the two because what we feel and what has actually happened can easily be mistaken. This is why it's important for us to place our full trust in God and never in what we think, feel, or see. Our complete dependence on God has the ability to take us to a new level of freedom and the longer we wait and try to do things on our own, the longer we will have to wait for the blessing of complete freedom. The truth is, God does not desire to be close to us because of what we can do for Him, but because of what He does for us in the most sacred and intimate moments of our lives. Sometimes we can stay stuck and confused because of the people who only wanted to take, but sisters, I plead with you to not diminish your value by keeping God out because of what someone else had done.

K.D. mentioned that God not only wants to heal us, but He also desires to help us. Do you know what that really means? It means that God is not trying to strip away our abilities or strength. He wants to maximize our capabilities as we rest and rely on Him. He wants to help us through what we've experienced so that we can indeed see the treasured gifts that we are. The lie of the enemy and the life of insecurity tells us that we will never make it, that we have fallen too many times for God to rescue us again and that because of our brokenness, we remain unfixable. But the devil is a liar, and there is nothing or no one who can stop us from walking in God's light and love. Dare to do what you've never done before. Turn around, fall straight back, and be held in God's arms. What a beautiful image, having the ability to fall back without fear, reservations, or regret. This is the life that God has promised to you, this is what you've been destined for; to rest and abide in Him as He abides in you.

Second Corinthians 4:7 is a reminder that though we are nothing more than fragile clay, but we have a great treasure on the inside, who is Christ. Because of Him, we can shine like the priceless jewels that we are. We don't have to compromise, bow, or bend. We can stand up for what is right and turn away from that which is wrong. If God is for us, then who can be against us (Romans 8:31)? There is no fear, and there is no turning back because God, your Father, is forever with you. He desires to cradle you in His arms and hold you just as a baby is rocked to sleep by their mother.

He wants to remove the stereotypes that have been placed on you. He wishes to eliminate the feelings of insecurity that have come with the challenges of your life. He desires to heal the hurt that comes when your voice is not heard, and your heart is not handled with care. This is a journey that is perfected with each new day and a journey that does not need to be rushed. God is with you always and what did not happen yesterday; God can certainly do today! You are on a journey with the King, and where He is preparing to take you, I guarantee you've never been before! There are many things that we've discussed throughout this book, but what God is getting ready to do in your heart and in your life will take you to a new level of freedom.

Throughout this book, we have opened our hearts, declared the Word of the Lord, and have also been challenged to make better decisions. Above all of these things, God desires for us to know His love as a Father. This may be hard for you if you have not had a father present in your life or if your father was not the best example. However, will you allow yourself to become vulnerable and opened before God? He calls you daughter and what love He has for you! Maybe you weren't daddy's little girl growing up, but it doesn't mean that you can't be daddy's little girl now. The love that God is about to pour on you in the next chapter will soften your heart, heal your hurt, and mend your brokenness. This is what happens when you are in the presence of the King. Life changes and healing takes place! Forever will God be with you and forever will He love you.

Everything that was once broken is made whole and complete in the presence of the King.

CHAPTER 9

The Mender of Broken Hearts

"He heals the brokenhearted and bandages their wounds." Psalm 147:3 (NLT)

The amazing thing about letting go and allowing God's love to flow is what happens in the process. Healing takes place as a result of letting go of what was and allowing God's love to flow into what is. We have all had our hearts broken at some time or another; either because of a failed relationship, a secret that was told, trust that was abused, or neglect that had taken place. The list actually goes on and on concerning the various ways that we come to a place of brokenness. However, in the midst of the variety of ways that we become broken, there is only one way for our hearts to be mended. That one way is a complete surrender to God.

The Bible speaks of the broken hearted, and this is what it says according to Psalm 34:18, "The Lord is close to the brokenhearted; he rescues those whose spirits are crushed" (NLT). This tells us that our brokenness does not distance us from God, it draws us to Him. God is not disappointed or shocked by the condition of your heart because He knows you and your story, and He knows He can mend all that is broken. Although, we must keep in mind that God also calls us to guard our heart. Our hearts are the keepers of our treasures, our emotions, and in many ways, our loyalty towards what we feel is right.

Proverbs 4:23 encourages us to "Guard your heart above all else, for it determines the course of your life" (NLT). Wow, my sister, how do you feel about that? Can you imagine that what's in your heart carries the weight of your future? This makes so much sense about the various scriptures throughout the Bible (c.f., Jeremiah 17:9) that speaks of the heart being deceitful, powerful, and can often lead us down the wrong path. How amazingly all-knowing and all-powerful is our Father that He made it clear that we must surrender our hearts to Him. As we do this, we open our lives up to the beauty of God's love, grace, and truth. It is only in Christ that we truly find healing. Throughout the Bible, Jesus is called the "Great Physician." Jesus is this, not just because He brought healing power with Him, but because He was "healing" (a real and tangible manifestation of God healing).

Proverbs says that we should guard our hearts above all else. Guarding our hearts can be a hard thing to do when you've met someone who you are interested in dating or whose time you appreciate on a consistent basis. There are variables in our lives that often cloud us from making the best decisions that we can make. However, our prayers being directed at God concerning our hearts being covered and our actions following that request give us stability and confidence that can only come from God.

You see, when you have a romantic interest in someone, your ability to make decisions that should be done with wisdom can often become clouded. This is why it's important to surrender everything daily to God, even the areas that we feel that we have under control. This is especially true when we don't have a clue of what we are doing. Now that we know the course of our lives is determined by the condition of the heart, what will we do differently? I remember as a teenager having crushes on guys and within a few days' time, praying to God and journaling about how I didn't want the guy to like me back because I decided that I only wanted to be his sister. I remember asking God to take the "I want to have a boyfriend" mentality away, so He did.

Now don't get me wrong, as a late teen and into my early 20's, I had lots of guy friends and some whom I found very attractive. However, in the depth of my heart, I was driven to pursue only God. In my mind, it was my way of taking control over my heart. But you know what happens when we take control? We lose control. When we give up control is when we then gain it in Christ (Luke 7:33). As Daughters of the King, it's important to know who we are, what we were created to do, and the role that God had given us even before we were in our mother's womb. When we surrender to what we don't have in our hands but what we see with our eyes, we are then living a life of faith and a life that has been given entirely to God.

On the other hand, there are decisions that we make that have the ability to change the course of our lives, just as the scripture said. In those moments we must hold on to the power and strength of God's unchanging hands. Sure, it won't be easy, but it will certainly be worth it. When you see that *you* are worth it (meaning worth it all), others begin to grab hold of that as well. How amazing would it be for us to start speaking positive words over our sisters and watching God maximize our decisions, making our one decision contagious to many? This is more of a reality than what we could ever imagine. In fact, more people are grabbing hold of the power of their words and using them as a tool for life.

Giving God the fragments of your heart that had been broken is like giving God a remote control whose batteries no longer work. In the same way, there is not a problem with the remote control only with what has been placed in it. In a similar way, your heart has not been damaged, but more so who and what you have allowed in, is what is causing all the problems. Your heart is fragile and as we said according to Jeremiah 17:9 we are reminded that, *"The human heart is the most deceitful of all things, and desperately wicked. Who really knows how bad it is" (NLT).* What we have to remember is that the human heart cannot be understood. This is why we aren't called as Christians to follow our hearts, but to follow Christ. We can't even fully understand the matters of the heart or when our heart is saying something different from our actions, or more importantly, from God's word. Anything that has the ability to confuse or contradict the truth needs to be placed under submission to God. This is why we must put our hearts, our minds, and our souls in the hands of the Father daily.

As long as we are keeping our ears open to the voice of God and not to the voice of others or even our own, we will have a clear direction. In life, many distractions would love to have our attention, but to not be distracted, we must be entirely consumed by something else or with someone else. In our lives, this should be relatively easy because before we enter into a relationship of any kind, we must be aware of the fact that it's God who holds the key to our hearts. Even if your heart has been broken, shattered into pieces, or stomped on, no hurt is too deeply set that God can not heal or mend.

The process of healing is a process that happens to the degree in which you allow it. Have you ever heard someone say, "The sore will never heal properly because you keep picking at it?" I'm sure you have. Maybe this was said to you long ago, and you never considered how relevant this was about the brokenness that is experienced today. I grew up believing that I was okay, only because I had ignored the situations or feelings that would, in some way, cause me to feel uncomfortable or lacked peace. In my mind, I was fine. I had an amazing private school education, my first car at 15, and later attending a school that only God could afford financially. I felt like I had made it through the hardship of my earlier days with experiencing neglect and always wanting a family like what I had seen on television. That is until I left home and headed to the Caribbean to serve a ministry there as a youth pastor. I didn't know that I had not given God all of my hurt until He confronted me with, "Give your parents a call and tell them how much you love them and are proud of them." I remember thinking to myself, "I've done this before. Do I really have to God?" But He made it clear to me that I was still holding on to the past, maybe not in a way that was noticeable, but certainly in a way that limited me. I was far from being able to love them God's way and not on my terms.

You see, often we feel like our hearts have been healed from the broken family, divorced parents, the rumor that ruined everything, or the people that we were ignored by, simply because we didn't talk about it or we still managed to smile. However, true healing is produced when we are able to look at adversity in the face and not be moved by it because we know that defeat is no longer an option. When we get to that place, without cringing, running away, backing down, or ignoring how we feel, then we know that healing, at a bare minimum, has begun to take root in our lives. There are stages of healing, and they don't happen overnight, but over time and once again to the degree in which we allow.

5 Stages of Healing

1. Acknowledge that brokenness exists. When we come out of denial about how we feel and what has happened, we open ourselves up to the healing power of God.

2. When we are willing, we need to take a step back from the hurt and assess what happened. When we have been hurt, it is often a challenge to clearly understand what has happened, so taking a few

steps back from the situation to gain a better view is important.

3. Make a decision to learn from the experience or wallow in it. Far too often we get stuck here because we feel that learning from negative experiences means that we are giving excuses what has been done; however, that couldn't be further from the truth. When we make the decision to learn from what has happened, we make the decisions we need to make to become empowered even in brokenness vs. being weakened and often discouraged.

4. Choose to forgive. Our choice to forgive is our choice to be free. Forgiving ourselves and forgiving others does not make what was done right, but it frees us from being stuck in what was done.

5. Move forward. Sometimes we follow steps 1-4 but refuse to move away from what happened. We end up constantly talking about it, crying about it, and become bitter because we have not actually moved forward. Moving forward allows you to walk in the fullness of who you are after the hurt and not who you were in the midst of pain.

Liberation is experienced when we let the chains go, and we welcome freedom. We all have experienced things that have shattered our views regarding our self-worth, our families, guys, dating, overall relationships, friendships, success, and our future. But you know, life is not about what we experience but how we choose to respond to our experiences. We are treasured daughters, and everything that we have experienced in our lives has been known by God. Though we doubt and often question where God was when it happened, the truth is the fact that we are still here is proof that God was indeed with us the whole time.

Maybe some of your dreams have been shattered, and maybe some of your hopes have been deferred, but right in the middle lies God's promises and every one of them is true. Jeremiah 1:12 speaks of God watching over His promises and declaring that everything He has said shall happen. This gives us confidence that when God had said something, it will come to be. I remind myself often that God is not like us; He doesn't say something today, change His mind tomorrow, and come up with something different the day after. Our Father is consistent, and He never changes. His words are true and no matter who told us that their words were true, but lied, we can still be rest assured that God always carries out His word.

Treasured

My sister, if your heart has never been healed or if you are currently experiencing hurt in your life I encourage you with these words:

My yesterday's pain will not hold me back from my right-now joy. I am stronger than I've ever been, and I am determined to be all that God's created me to be. I am determined to do all that God desires for me to do and I have made up in my mind that my life will no longer be put on hold because of grudges or anger that I am carrying. Today, I give it to you Father, and I know that no matter how shattered my heart may be, you alone can take all of the pieces and mend them. I refuse to stay where I was because I now know that there is more to me. I will not allow myself to remain offended by what my friends did, said, or thought. I am only allowing positivity in my life, and I know that this must start with me. I know that you have so much for me Father, and today I step out of the box and trust you with my whole heart. I am complete, not because of what people tell me or what I am currently doing, but because you created me as a whole and I am fearfully and wonderfully made. I am a Daughter of the King, and I know who I am. I am free. I am completely yours. I am new, and I am healed. I am, because of you. Amen.

May you continue to embrace who you are, because who you are not is insignificant and who you are becoming is in the making. Remind one of your sisters today that they are a DOTK and nothing that has happened yesterday or today can change that.

> *"A good person produces good things from the treasury of a good heart, and an evil person produces evil things from the treasury of an evil heart. What you say flows from what is in your heart." (Luke 6:45 NLT)*

Guard your heart as you surrender it to God daily and keep in mind that what is in your heart will come out in your words. So, even in the moments where you are trying to figure out "where that came from," know that it came from within. David said in Psalm 51:10, "Create in me a clean heart." This is what God does when He takes the shattered pieces of our hearts. He is the mender of the broken-hearted; He is the mender of you and me.

The shattered fragments of your heart today will be a masterpiece of God's love, grace, and favor tomorrow. Tomorrow will come and bring in a new day.

CHAPTER 10

Where Is Your Treasure?

"Wherever your treasure is, there the desires of your heart will also be." Matthew 6:21 (NLT)

This scripture has great meaning and purpose to me. It has had an impact on how I live. I have some treasures on earth like my family, my Bible, and my friends; but especially Jesus! Matthew 6:19-21 says to not store up treasures on earth but in Heaven. This verse tells me that my heart will follow after my treasure. This means to me that where I spend my time, my money, my effort, and my thoughts reflect what's in my heart. When I read this scripture, I am reminded of the man who spent all that he had on a precious pearl because that's what he treasured. But today I ask you, "Where do you spend all your time, money, effort, and thoughts?" This will prove where your heart is.

Natasha Jang, Treasured Girl

Have you ever been so excited to buy something but once you got it home, used it, played with it, or wore it the excitement wore off? I know I have. I remember buying my first car and not allowing people to eat in it at all. I had a "no wrapper" policy, which meant anything that had a wrapper could not be eaten in my car. Talk about storing your treasure on earth! I was doing that without a second thought. I had become extremely materialistic during that stage of my life. I would buy clothes and shoes literally every week, saving very little. I know that for most of us, our appearance is a big deal and unfortunately it becomes much greater than the condition of our hearts. For me, it was no different, but I thank God for change, growth, and maturity.

Jesus is saying that when we find joy, fulfillment, and in some ways, complete wholeness in that which has no eternal value, we are selling ourselves short. I can say this to you because I have been there and have done that. I am thankful that God had given me a new understanding regarding what it means to be treasured. It's interesting what Natasha said about where we place our attention regarding our treasures. We may think we've had our priorities straight, but the truth is, we couldn't be further from the truth. If we are honest with ourselves, we have been guilty of investing more into how we look than what we put in our relationship with God, character, or overall love for people. Any time this is the case, we have identified through action where our hearts are.

We may be able to fool people regarding what we think is important, but we can't escape God nor can we escape the reality of where our attention lies. I love how Natasha listed her treasures and how they were family-oriented and rooted in her foundation in God. It is easy to forget the joy and privilege of having loved ones surround us constantly or a real tangible relationship with God. However, may this chapter challenge you to dig deeper than before. Take a moment and write down your treasures. List the top 5 priorities that you have right now, that you treasure the most. What do you see? Is your list filled with people that have eternal value or relationships that have been created during artificial seasons of your life? You know the seasons, where you hang on to people because of loneliness or insecurities and have somehow convinced yourself that it's not that way?! You've never done that ever! No, definitely not you! All jokes aside; you probably have.

As you look at your list of treasures, what do you see? Do you see a reflection of something that far exceeds today, right now, your age, or the school that you attend, or job that you have? Is your list based on things that can never be taken away or diminished with time? Look at what Matthew 6:20 says, "Store your treasures in heaven, where moths and rust cannot destroy, and thieves do not break in and steal" (NLT). If this isn't warning us of the temporary gain and temporary worth that we often overlook, then I don't know what is. We are being warned and informed that there would be things that grab our attention, but have no eternal value, yet we will be lured into holding on to these things by our own selfish nature and the enemy.

I'm sure there have been things in your life that you once valued, but once you invited Christ into your heart, your life and values started to be defined by other things. This is what happens when you give God complete control. Just as I shared my personal account of storing my treasures here on earth and the turn around that happened for me, you too must decide that which had taken up space in your heart and does not belong there.

The Treasure Box of Our Hearts

- Our treasures should bring out the beauty of who we are as a person rooted in Christ.

- Our treasures should reflect eternal value.

- Our treasures should not be temporary.

- Our treasures should not be based on what people have said to us or about us.

- Our treasures should inspire the people around us.

- Our treasures should not distract us from doing God's work.

- Our treasures should not be created out of lack, void, or insecurity.

- Our treasures should always make us a better person.

- Our treasures should not define who we are.

- Our treasures should play a role in building God's Kingdom.

- Our treasures should be based on the promises of God and not man.

- Our treasures should always encourage us and not leave us feeling "less than."

- Our treasures should ultimately be a form of worship unto God.

- Our treasures should not draw us away from God, but draw us toward Him instead.

- Our treasures should give us something to look forward to.

- Our treasures should remind us of how treasured we are in God's eyes.

- Our treasures should never be more important than the box in which they are carried; our hearts.

Whatever you long for the most will be where your heart is. In this way, you can be in a crowded room but be completely shut off from what is going on around you because that which you treasure is where your heart and mind will be. There may be times in your life where you feel limited by the things that hold your attention because of the desires that you have, but in many ways I think that this is a reminder that whatever we hold dear will be the very thing that remains on our mind no matter what. In and of itself this is not a bad thing. However, it can indeed turn into one when our treasures are placed in things that are not eternal.

Treasures can be hard to find. But, they are just as much of a challenge to keep once they are found; especially when they are being stored on earth. According to the scripture that Natasha shared, we are challenged by the Word to store our treasures in heaven. The treasures that have eternal value are identified in many ways like on the *Treasure Box of our Hearts* list. When we are able to identify the treasures of our heart and are able to consider what treasures are eternal and what treasures are earthly, we begin to understand how often we look for personal value based on our treasures. Like for me, my treasures revolved around my vehicle, my clothes, and anything else I could buy. But when you understand your worth and value as a treasured daughter, life looks a whole lot different.

I won't say this is an easy process because it is a daily decision to choose eternal treasures over earthly gain. I would be lying to you if I said I don't buy the occasional pair(s) of shoes and have to later return them and repent. There are days where I think to myself, if only I had this or if only I had that, but then God speaks in a small, gentle voice reminding me that great is my treasure in Heaven. You see, when we don't know what is waiting for us we feel like we need to rush, make things happen, or indulge in things that will profit us very little. However, when we fully begin to recognize and accept that God has amazing things planned for us, we no longer have to make things happen or fill a void. God desires for us to live life on cruise control, meaning we are the ones cruising, and He is the one behind the wheel. There are no limits to what God can do when we step aside and get out of the driver's seat.

Defining our treasures and eliminating an "I want it now" mentality will save us a lot of heartaches, headaches, money, and time. Having a clear understanding of what God has planned for you and what you believe by faith is the beginning of establishing your treasures in things that are eternal. *You don't have to rush when you know what's waiting for you.* You don't have to create things when you know your life is in the palm of His hand. You are free to live the life that has been given, free to no longer live in the shadows of fear of losing your treasures because God is the keeper of all things precious. God is the keeper of you and me.

I can't begin to explain to you the joy that comes when you know you are right where God wants you, and everything that you need is at your fingertips. To say the least, the joy is overflowing, it is constant, and the peace that God gives you when you trust Him in this way is beyond amazing. God will not withhold anything good from you. It's comforting being able to know that and to believe it with your whole heart. The love that God has for you and the plan that He has for your life is not because you are so good, it's because He is so gracious. God is not searching for "good" people to bless. He is searching for those who have surrendered to Him even in the midst of making decisions that aren't always the best.

No matter what you've done up to this point and no matter what your treasures were before reading this book or even this chapter, God desires to wow you with His very best. Exchange what once was and give it over to God. There is nothing to lose in Him, only gain. It is His will that we prosper according to Jeremiah 29:11. This means that God desires the best, and when our eyes are opened to His best, we will never want to settle for less. I know this may come as a surprise to you, but even in decisions that were made regarding treasures that were temporary, God can turn it around. Just because you have invested time into something that had no eternal value does not mean that God can't turn it around and have it work for your good. According to Romans 8:28, God causes all things to work together for the good of them that love Him and are called according to His purpose.

You see God is not limited by what we've experienced. He works above and beyond what we could ever imagine. In many ways, God is saying to us, "Give me the situation and I will show you how I am the solution." He doesn't say, "I will *give* you the solution," instead He says, "I will *be* your solution." The amazing thing about God is that He doesn't present options; He simply presents Himself as the way. There is nothing that we've experienced in this life that can separate us from God's plan for us. The desires of your heart are ever present before the Lord and though it may seem like God is slow in responding to your desires, He is not. "The Lord isn't really being slow about his promises, as some people think. No, he is being patient for your sake. He does not want anyone to be destroyed but wants everyone to repent" (2 Peter 3:9 NLT).

Your desires are valid, your dreams are valid, and the treasures that are being prepared for you exceed anything that you could imagine here on earth. Your worth and value are not defined by what you have here on earth. Your worth and value are determined by what you are willing to let go of, for God to fill you with more of Him. It's not about what you've gained; it's what you gave. The Bible says, "Give, and you will receive. Your gift will return to you in full—pressed down, shaken together to make room for more, running over, and poured into your lap. The amount you give will determine the amount you get back" (Luke 6:38 NLT).

The treasures of your heart are a reflection of your desires. Your desires are a reflection of your priorities. Your priorities are a reflection of God's role in your life!

CHAPTER 11

But I love Him

"Guard your heart above all else, for it determines the course of your life." Proverbs 4:23 (NLT)

I remember, just like it was yesterday, I was in my senior year of high school and had started dating for the first time. There was nothing that anyone could tell me. I was convinced that this would be my husband even if I had to make it work. In many ways, I felt like my heart was in it, but as I look back today, eleven years into the future, I realize that my heart was no longer guarded but open and vulnerable. You see, I had dreamed that my first boyfriend would be my husband, and I had told many people that very statement my entire life. I was the one that my friends would go to for relationship advice because I had always been firm on my "no dating as a high school student" policy. I guess in many ways that led my friends to believe that there was some possible wisdom that I had attained in my decision to abstain from such.

However, the truth is, once you open your heart to someone, you become susceptible to hurt and pain. There is just no way around it. Of course, I would like to believe that no one enters into a relationship with the intent of hurting the other person, but time and time again we learn that hurt is a part of our experience on our journey through life. There is no way to avoid what happens when you feel like you really like someone or even love them. There is a point you get to, where no one can tell you anything, and you have to learn those life lessons on your own, sometimes the hard way. I know that I had to. I remember reading Proverbs 4:23 and also hearing people refer to it as well, but didn't fully understand the significance until I realized that I had done the very opposite.

This scripture is not just telling us to guard our hearts for the purpose of protection but to guard our hearts so that ultimately we are not hardened or tainted by things experienced during the time we left our hearts exposed. The truth is, when we become blind to the clear and present reality because our emotions are involved, we will always find ourselves in the dark. The reason is this if we were to admit what's wrong in the pursuit, the relationship, the boundaries; it would mean that we would be held accountable for those decisions. As I was preparing to graduate from high school, I had new emotions that I had never experienced before, feelings that I didn't know existed and, in many ways, I felt lost to all that was happening.

My particular choice of a first boyfriend was far from what my family thought to be a suitable choice for me. Up to that point I felt like so much of my life had been structured and neat, and this guy was everything that I wasn't; spontaneous, hilarious, no filter, and in many ways child-like. You see, I spent the first 22 years of my life being solemn about my life and my personal journey. After a certain few events, life started to take on a new form. That new form began when I opened my heart for the first time. I remember falling asleep on the phone and never wanting to admit that I was tired. However, I also remember knowing deep within that this "first boyfriend" was not going to be my husband.

I tried so very hard to convince myself, my family, and my friends, but everyone knew what I refused to see. He just wasn't "the one." In many ways, we try and accommodate the lack that we see in our relationships to fill a void that can only be filled by God. In fact, in John 4:14 Jesus says, "But those who drink the water I give will never be thirsty again. It becomes a fresh, bubbling spring within them, giving them eternal life." Jesus was saying here that we can get a drink from many springs that are made available (guys, jobs, education, money, to name a few) but there is only one spring that has the ability to quench and satisfy our thirst. Maybe you are how I was as a teenager, trying to fill a round hole with a square peg. You've pushed, pleaded, begged, and squeezed someone into your life that has created an artificial filler that, in the end, leaves you thirstier than what you were in the beginning.

This is not a judgment. I have been there and have done that. I remember telling my grandma on many occasions that "I love him, and you just don't understand, you don't know him like I do." She would say to me in response, "Miracle, I don't need to know him, I can see all that I need to see from where I am standing." But you know, I was not taking her word for it, or anyone else's for that matter. That is until God grabbed ahold of me. I remember thinking that if everyone is seeing something that I'm not, maybe I need to adjust the lens which I am looking through. I prayed after more than a year of dating, inconsistently arguing and stressing for God to reveal to me everything that I needed to see, and He did.

Those secret things in our heart and deeds that have been hidden can only stay in darkness for a while and after that, everything that had been hidden will come to light. For me, that is exactly what happened. God began to uncover things that had been present the whole time, but because my heart wasn't ready to receive nor were my eyes ready to see truth, those things remained hidden. I'll say that again to you my sisters if you have to convince yourself or defend the relationship that you are in, most of the time you are running from the hidden things that remain in darkness. This is not God's will for us as Daughters of the King, neither is it God's will for His sons to allow themselves to settle because of what the fellas are saying.

At the end of the day, we must be willing to place our desires at the feet of Jesus, trusting and believing that God will not withhold anything good from us. God declares throughout the Bible that His promises are true, meaning that everything that God has for you is indeed for you, and it is good. There will be things in this life that you will have to fight over, yell over, run past, or make happen. But what God has for you is yours, you don't have to fight for it, it's freely given. The challenge often comes when we look at our girlfriends and their relationships and somehow think that we are less than or not good enough because we don't have what they have. However, do you know that everything in this life that has great significance and great worth takes time and a little bit of Jesus?

The greatly missed and highly-respected Dr. Maya Angelou once said, "A woman's heart should be so hidden in God that a man has to seek Him just to find her." What an image! We as Daughters of the King should be seeking God more than anything or anyone else. Our desire should be to stand in the ultimate position that God wants for us because in His presence, there is a fullness of joy and at His right hand, there are pleasures forevermore (Psalm 16:11). Everything that our heart yearns for is found in the presence of the King and the relationships we have, at times, serve as artificial fillers that could never take God's place. Now, don't get me wrong ladies, I am a single adult woman, and I believe in the beauty, purpose, love, honor, and value that's found in covenantal marriage. I believe that marriage and intimacy that is created between husband and wife is the closest and most dynamic example that we have of Christ loving us. In fact, Ephesians 5:25 speaks of a husband's love being likened unto Christ loving the church. However, I am illustrating to you with Dr. Angelou's quote that our first love is Christ, and as we seek Him first, everything else comes into perfect alignment (exactly how and when God has planned for it to be).

Maintaining and consistently grooming the relationship with the Father prepares you for every other relationship in your life. If we don't take out time to truly know who we are in Him, we will never know who we are with them (our significant other). It's important for us, as daughters, to grab hold of the best example of love that we have, which is found in Christ giving His life for us. We see throughout all of scripture that God loved us first and that He made it very clear that His love was one way. He didn't wait for us to love Him back. He made the first move, and He continued to get closer and closer. First John 4:10 says, "This is real love—not that we loved God, but that he loved us and sent his Son as a sacrifice to take away our sins" (NLT). This kind of love is the love that will flow in and through us as we seek God with our whole heart. It is this kind of perfect love that moves us from what we want, what we think we need, and who we believe we love, to a place of authentic, unwavering love that is selfless and perfect in His timing.

Jeremiah 29:13 puts it this way, "You will seek me and find me when you seek me with all your heart" (NLT). My issue wasn't that I refused to seek God regarding who I should allow in my life. My issue was that I had one eye looking in God's direction and the other eye looking in the direction of my heart's desire—which, if you recall, we learned that our hearts are deceptive. It's common to only see what you want to see when you know that seeing the truth and the reality of what's going on could have a hurtful impact on ourselves. But the best thing you can do is seek your truth from God and not from your desires or your dreams. The truth is found in Christ alone, and when we refuse to see that truth, we are choosing to be willingly and willfully ignorant. I have decided to live in darkness by choice.

Maybe, at this very moment, you are reading this chapter and knowing in your heart that you are in a relationship that does not motivate you to be all that you can be for God and through God. The only thing you are being motivated to be is what will please that person. Don't allow the momentary comfort and artificial feeling of complete wholeness keep you from the truth. As a teenager, I knew that God had a plan for my life and one day for my marriage. I also knew that the decisions that I made then could affect my overall destiny. A decade later, I am able to share with you the importance of seeking God as the ultimate source of your joy and complete fulfillment. Of course, we like to be complimented and talked sweetly to and there is nothing wrong with that. However, we must also guard our hearts no matter how much you may feel or think that you love him (that guy in your life or the one that you wish was in your life).

There are many lessons learned as we seek God for wisdom, and the most important thing that we must remember is that all things are perfect in God's timing. There is nothing like rushing into a relationship because you're watching the #relationshipgoals of others. When you take your eyes off of the portion (life) that God has given you and begin to desire what someone else has, it is a recipe for disaster. Now, I know that it can be tempting to want what someone else has, depending on your age, your goal as a wife/girlfriend, and or a mother. However, we can't allow ourselves to be thrown into the pool of lies from the enemy, causing us to believe that we are limited because of time, our age, our friends, or pictures that people post on social media. I learned some time ago that at the end of the day, you are living your life for the fulfillment of who you are in Christ, not for the fulfillment of others. This is a truth that we must consistently be willing to acknowledge and commit to. The time we take to establish our relationship with God will be the foundation by which all other relationships are laid.

To everything, there is a season and in that season what is meant to be will be. Song of Songs 8:4 says, "Promise me, O women of Jerusalem, not to awaken love until the time is right." This can be a challenge when your eyes have been turned on to the amazing smile, physique, or humor of the guy who has caught your eye. In God, we should realize that not only is it our responsibility to guard our heart, but we must also protect the hearts of our brothers in Christ with our actions. Have you ever conveyed something to a guy and he completely took it in a way that you did not mean? Or have you ever (now, be honest) left your house dressed a bit "sexy" because of the attention that you received the last time you wore those jeans or that dress? I know these things may seem like small things, but anytime we adjust our standards or our behavior, our stance for Christ, and our guard is being affected and even lowered.

In all of our hearts, we desire to be loved and to love, and I love what the Bible says according to 1 John 4:7-19.

"Dear friends, let us continue to love one another, for love comes from God. Anyone who loves is a child of God and knows God. But anyone who does not love does not know God, for God is love. God showed how much he loved us by sending his one and only Son into the world so that we might have eternal life through him. This is real love—not that we loved God, but that he loved us and sent his Son as a sacrifice to take away our sins. Dear friends, since God loved us that much, we surely ought to love each other. No one has ever seen God. But if we love each other, God lives in us, and his love is brought to full expression in us. And God has given us his Spirit as proof that we live in him and he in us. Furthermore, we have seen with our own eyes and now testify that the Father sent his Son to be the Savior of the world. All who declare that Jesus is the Son of God have God living in them, and they live in God. We know how much God loves us, and we have put our trust in his love. God is love, and all who live in love live in God, and God lives in them. And as we live in God, our love grows more perfect. So we will not be afraid on the day of judgment, but we can face him with confidence because we live like Jesus here in this world. Such love has no fear because perfect love expels all fear. If we are afraid, it is for fear of punishment,

*and this shows that we have not fully experienced his perfect
love. We love each other because he loved us first." (NLT)*

What an amazing picture of what God gives and also
of what we are called to give as well. Our ability to love
comes not from our emotions, based on what we see
outwardly or admire. Our ability to love comes from God,
and as we grow in Him first, our love then becomes more
perfect. This is the defining factor by which we are able to
properly love and give our hearts to another; when we first
surrender to God. Don't ever think for a second that the love
you have for your interest could ever do more for you than
what God can provide. In fact, what you feel for "him" is a
reflection of the love that comes from Him (God). Take time
to fully understand your worth and value in Christ and sit
at His feet, basking in His presence, being filled with His
love so that you will be able to give the love that comes from
Him to "him." There is such purity and honesty in love that
comes from God, and when you know it's from God,
nothing can stand in the way. Continue to do all that you
can today, fully appreciating and embracing your right now
while thanking God in advance for the beautiful things to
come.

You may have told everyone that it would work out
with this one. You may have even convinced yourself, like I
had years ago, that this guy would one day be your

husband. But life has a way of showing us what we really need to see and learn. Who knows, maybe the guy you like will one day be your Mr. Forever, but for today allow God be your right now and always. It doesn't matter what happened or what you've done, God can and will bring healing to your hurt and give you the strength to move forward in Him and with Him, only if you let Him. I know you may be trying really hard to convince yourself, your family, and maybe even your guy that this will last forever because you love him. However, when you release your desires into the hands of God, there are no limits to what God can do! You are on your way, on a journey, that will place a smile on your face not because of what you've been given but because of who you are. Guarding your heart is not trusting the feelings that you have, but trusting the God you know!

Remember that the greatest gift you can give to someone is the authentic you and a perfect love that has been established in your relationship with God.

CHAPTER 12

Confession

"Therefore confess your sins to each other and pray
for each other so that you may be healed. The prayer
of a righteous person is powerful and effective."
James 5:16

My soul was no longer devoted to the one, true and living God, but to my own selfish motives. I was casting myself into the pit of my own destruction. I dreamed of oblivion, and my soul screamed in agony. I had given up on myself. I believed I was worthless so that is how I treated myself. I was completely and utterly depressed, and when someone is depressed they usually find some form of addiction, mine was pornography and using sex toys. I have no deeper regret during this time spent away from God doing evil to myself and others. No one who loved me knew except God. I was born and raised in a Christian home but when my parents divorced God was forgotten. My entire family had been depressed and broken. I had no one to turn to except the only one who could save me, and I had forgotten Him. I went to Bible camp for a week in the summer. It was like when you try to see underwater and your eyes sting, and everything is blurry, and then your head comes up and everything is clear again. I came to God, and He just hugged me and cried with me. He wasn't angry or harsh, He just loved me! It wasn't all better instantly, and the pain wasn't all gone, but my soul was resurrected.

For the first time in what felt like forever, I could feel the hurt, pain, anger, regret, and shame, but I could also feel HOPE! God has been shaping me like a potter would a vase ever since. Though God was with me and I was better than I was, I still had a great weight on my heart; my mom. I had always told her everything until the divorce. I thought she would be ashamed of me and lash out at me with anger. For me, the thought that my mom would find out paralyzed me with fear and shame. The devil used this fear and lie to control me and to keep me in the dark. The evil one told me I was to be ashamed of myself and hate myself for what I'd done. But NO! God had forgiven me and the second I had asked I was His child, and He was not ashamed of me. God told me what I needed to say, and I kind of told Him that He was crazy, but I knew He was asking because He wanted to heal me. I talked to a very prominent Christian adult who had recently shown up in my life, who I had already confided in. She didn't tell me what to do, but just prayed with me and helped me focus on God. A few days later I told my Mom. While I talked, she just nodded her head and listened, and she gave me a big hug and told me she loved me and was not ashamed of me and told me she was sorry for not being there for me. What a wave of healing passed through me! Praise the Lord! Even if my mom weren't the wonderful, beautiful, and amazing person she is, God would've still have blessed me for obeying.

The devil relishes in secrecy because it creates shame and so many other things that he can use to manipulate people and whisper lies. I have now told my testimony to my sisters and brothers in Christ, my mom, my class

(Scary!), and now you. It doesn't have to be your parents who you hide from, just trust in God! GOD LOVES YOU! Never let the enemy tell you otherwise! God is still shaping me and healing me with every hour. I am so grateful for God for everything He has done and is continuing to do. I love Him! He has resurrected me. GLORY TO HIM, THE MOST-HIGH! No words I could ever say would do Him justice. I could say, "Holy! Holy! is He, all glory is given to Him, for all eternity," and it would never be enough! God, I give my life to you. Guide me so I can walk with you all of my days and never stop praising you! You are great, and there is no heart more loving or healing than yours. The time spent without Him cannot be excused, but God has certainly redeemed the time. He will not judge you harshly, but instead give you the biggest hug ever!

He loves you and me more than we could ever know.

Rose Hope, Treasured Girl

What a powerful testimony of God's love, redemption, and forgiveness. I sit amazed at what God has done and continually does in the life of this Treasured Girl. It doesn't matter what you've wrestled with in your life, God can turn things around for you. We talked a few chapters ago about the secret and hidden places of our hearts and how God desires to unveil them while the enemy tries to keep those things concealed. What power shared in this testimony of no longer hiding and no longer running! The very thing the enemy wanted her to do, God gave her the strength and courage to stop. You too can stop. It's your decision and it's the freedom that has been given to you by God. It doesn't matter how hidden your secrets or struggles may be, God is a God of forgiveness, and He loves you unconditionally.

Don't believe the lie that you are too far gone or that you have done too many things to be forgiven of. This is what God says to us today, "If my people, which are called by my name, shall humble themselves, and pray, and seek my face, and turn from their wicked ways; then will I hear from heaven, and will forgive their sin, and will heal their land" (2 Chronicles 7:14). God desires to heal those places that have been hidden for far too long. He wants to free you from the guilt and weight of it all. It's not His will for us to carry the burden of sin when He has already done that for us (John 3:16). Give every struggle to Him and allow Him to heal you. It's not about what people will think of you or even what your family would say, it's about receiving the love that comes from God, which covers a multitude of sin.

It has been mentioned time and time again that no one is perfect. But, the truth is, our imperfection is neither an excuse nor a reason for us to stay where we are when God's love brings change. Did you see how Rose shared that God did not judge, or condemn her? He wrapped His arms around her and loved her. You see, it's not guilt that changes us, it's love. The testimony we heard captures various things but one of the most interesting aspects of this testimony is that just as much as the enemy wanted to keep her quiet, God gave her boldness to speak up and to declare freedom. The Bible says that we overcome by the word of our testimony (Revelation 12:11). That means that when we release and let go of who we were and welcome who God is molding us to be, we are empowered and strengthened.

You don't have to feel ashamed of what you've done or even the things that have been wrongfully done to you. God loves you right where you are. You are His Treasured Daughter and His love for you flows like a river. The shame that you may be holding onto is a trap that the enemy loves to use against us, but at this very moment, I speak shame off of you in Jesus' name. You are who God has created you to be, and every sin that you have turned away from has been forgiven. God exchanges the shame and hurt that you are feeling with His love and acceptance. You are valuable, far more valuable than what the eye can see. Don't underestimate your worth and value because of what people have said about you or even what you have said about yourself. You serve a God, who provides so many chances for us to get it right, for us to turn every desire that is not like Him over.

You don't have to stay stuck in the shame, in the guilt, or even in the memories. You can be free; you can choose freedom right now at this moment. It doesn't matter if you were sexually active yesterday, today, or an hour ago; at this moment you can give it all over to God and turn away. You may not have struggled with what Rose has shared, but maybe it's your thoughts, the music that fills a void of loneliness, the conversations had with people, or maybe even inappropriate pictures sent or received. Whatever your hidden struggle may be, God can free you right now. In this very moment, I encourage you to declare these words and invite God in to heal, free, and deliver!

> Father, I know that I am yours and that you hold my life in the palm of your hand, but there have been moments where I've taken matters into my own hands and have done things that bring shame to me as well as my body. I know that this is not what you have for me. That you desire for my heart and actions to be pure. So, at this moment, I give my secrets, and hidden struggles over to you and I ask for your forgiveness and your strength to no longer live this way. I desire more than anything to live a life that is in accordance with the plan that you have for me, so I remove myself out of the way, and I ask you, Lord, to have your way with me. I have run and hidden for too long, and I am tired of hiding. I want freedom for my life. I want you in my life God, and I want to let go of everything that has held me back.
>
> Help me see who I am in you and not who I am in sin. I feel like I don't have people who I can trust with these things because I feel like I will be judged. I ask you,

Confession

Lord, to send Godly women into my life who will hold me accountable and who will help me along my journey of freedom. I thank you for welcoming me with open arms and for helping me to see that I am not unworthy because of anything that I have done. Your love and forgiveness carries me through. I declare that I am forgiven, free, and fearless. I will not spend another day bound by what was! I declare this is a new day and a new beginning for me.

Now, you may be thinking to yourself that there is no way that you can be changed in an instant. However, we see throughout scripture that people who called out to God were often freed instantly from their sin or illness. Freedom is not a one-time decision, it is something we choose daily. There will be moments when temptation comes, but be reminded that according to 1 Corinthians 10:13, God always provides a way of escape. Your freedom rests upon your daily decision to choose God's will. This will not be easy, but it will be worth every tear and every no. Your spiritual freedom is worth it all!

Walking in freedom and walking in forgiveness is being willing to acknowledge when you are in a situation that has the potential of leading you down a path that you no longer want to go down. If that means leaving someone's home early, not hanging out with certain people, or being very protective over your mind concerning what you watch and listen to, do it. There is nothing like desiring freedom but remaining in chains. You have the ability to break free just as Rose did and just as God gave her boldness, God can do the same for you. Don't look down on yourself because God certainly doesn't. He loves you relentlessly, and He will not give up on you.

Once you welcome Christ into your heart and into the hidden secrets, you are welcoming a new life. "This means that anyone who belongs to Christ has become a new person. The old life is gone; a new life has begun" 2 Corinthians 5:17 (NLT). How refreshing it is to know that when you step into Christ, you become new? You aren't who you were yesterday. You aren't who you were in sin because you are now who you are supposed to be in Christ. You are no longer held back from what was, you are free and complete in Him. People will try to tell you that you are the same, and maybe you will begin to think that you are but be assured YOU ARE NOT. There are no more chains. There are no longer any links keeping you in that place of bondage and sin. Live the life that has been created by the Father and maintained by His strength.

The thoughts of condemnation that will try and creep on you are traps from the enemy, so speak against every lie and word of defeat. No one is worthy in and of themselves, for we all have been saved by God's grace alone. Our salvation and our freedom are not predicated upon what we can do but by what we allow God to do in and through us.

Romans 3:20-26:

"For no one can ever be made right with God by doing what the law commands. The law simply shows us how sinful we are. But now God has shown us a way to be made right with him without keeping the requirements of the law, as was promised in the writings of Moses and the prophets long ago. We are made right with God by placing our faith in Jesus Christ. And this is true for everyone who believes, no matter who we are. For everyone has sinned; we all fall short of God's glorious standard. Yet God freely and graciously declares that we are righteous. He did this through Christ Jesus when he freed us from the penalty for our sins. For God presented Jesus as the sacrifice for sin. People are made right with God when they believe that Jesus sacrificed his life, shedding his blood. This sacrifice shows that God was being fair when he held back and did not punish those who sinned in times past, for he was looking ahead and including them in what he would do in this present time. God did this to demonstrate his righteousness, for he himself is fair and just, and he declares sinners to be right in his sight when they believe in Jesus." (NLT)

Paul is saying we are not made right with God because of all of the good that we do, the activities that we participate in, or by trying to make up for our sin by good works. There is no one walking this earth who has never sinned or who will never sin again. However, God, in His amazing grace and love for us, does not condemn us for our sin. He shows us a better way. As we place our faith in Jesus, our lives begin to change because we welcome His forgiveness in living a freed life. This means that we don't continue to run back to what was once our struggle, we submit this fight to God, thanking Him for giving us the power to overcome. Romans chapters 6 through 8 speak of the life-giving Spirit that comes from God and how this life-giving Spirit gives us the power to overcome and fight against sin.

Luke 3:8 says to, "Prove by the way you live that you have repented of your sins and turned to God. Don't just say to each other, 'We're safe, for we are descendants of Abraham.' That means nothing, for I tell you, God can create children of Abraham from these very stones." This means don't just think that you are okay because you belong to God. Show the world, show God, and show yourself that you have turned away from the way you have lived. I love this scripture because it is a reminder that God is not concerned with what we say. He is looking at what we are doing and how we represent Him daily. It doesn't matter if we've been in church our whole lives, if our family includes ministers, or even if we are involved in ministry; God is looking at the daily lifestyle that we live.

We can't overcome or fight in our own strength but in our daily surrender to God, we become stronger. He strengthens us to do far more than what we could do on our own. In the next chapter, I challenge you to consider the people, entertainment, relationships, and interests that play a role in the life that God has called you to as His daughter. Anything that moves us away from purity and encourages participating in a level of gratification that is only to take place with the marriage relationship is a sin. I will share my personal journey as an adult virgin and my struggle towards purity even in the midst of remaining a virgin. Get ready, because we are about to embark upon a journey that can change everything about our views of love, lust, relationships, dating, and physical boundaries. You have already declared your freedom and your detachment from that which has kept you stuck; now I invite you to pledge your purity as a Daughter of the King. Keep in mind that it doesn't matter what you've done in the past, God has freed you and has given you a new start in Him.

May you live a life of freedom, being reminded that Jesus paid it all so that we wouldn't have to! Freedom is the life that has been promised!

CHAPTER 13

The Purity Pledge

"How can a young (or old) person stay pure? By
obeying your word." Psalm 119:9 (NLT)

There is a battle that everyone must face and that battle
is to remain pure when it seems like all roads are leading in
the opposite direction. David is answering a question on
how to maintain purity. But first, we must understand that
purity is not limited to sex. It also includes conversations
that lead to inappropriate content (those late-night
conversations), movies that feed a spirit of lust (which
entertains the thought or act of sexual pleasure, and the
hidden sin that often remains in the closet—masturbation
(sexual self-gratification /pleasure). All of these things open
a door into our thought life and day to day living. These
behaviors and thoughts lead to brokenness, shame, and hurt
when not given to God. This is not God's will for His
daughters or for His sons.

There is nothing like fighting for what you know is right but wrestling with what you know is wrong, and yet know that engaging in the wrong brings temporary satisfaction. It's no mystery that we live in a "sex-driven" and even "sex-crazed" society. We see it everywhere. From the commercials on the television, to billboards, to music videos, and more prevalently, in the movies. But, what I've learned is that we are not tempted by closed doors, we are always tempted by doors that have been opened in our lives. Now, you may be thinking, "I just spoke against everything that had me trapped and everything that I used to do. Does that mean those doors that were opened remain open?" That is a great question, and my response to that is yes and no. Doors do not shut on their own, and in the same way, they do not open on their own. We've made decisions in our lives that have opened several doors whether it has to do with bad eating habits, lust, or profanity. To close those doors, we must confront them not only with our words but also with our actions.

I know that the world presents these things as a way of life and as if everyone is participating in these vices, but it's simply not the truth. God has created our bodies to be temples where He dwells, a place of purity and a place of worship. Romans 12: 1-2 says, "And so, dear brothers and sisters, I plead with you to give your bodies to God because of all he has done for you. Let them be a living and holy sacrifice—the kind he will find acceptable. This is truly the way to worship him. Don't copy the behavior and customs of this world, but let God transform you into a new person by changing the way you think. Then you will learn to know God's will for you, which is good and pleasing and perfect" (NLT). Paul said it perfectly! It doesn't matter what anyone else is doing, God desires for us, as His children, to submit and surrender our bodies to Him! This means that no one has a say over your body. This includes you and me. Our bodies do not belong to us when we have made a commitment to surrender our bodies to Christ.

"Don't you realize that your body is the temple of the Holy Spirit, who lives in you and was given to you by God? You do not belong to yourself, for God bought you with a high price. So you must honor God with your body" 1 Corinthians 6:19-20 (NLT).You may be thinking, "Well how unfair is that? We've been given bodies, and yet we can't control or have a say over what we do with them." This, I imagine to be a common thought, but when I read 1Corinthians 10:23, that *"I have the right to do anything," you say—but not everything is beneficial. 'I have the right to do anything'—but not everything is constructive."* I see God not trying to keep something good from me. I see God reminding me that though I have freedom to choose whatever I want, my freedom to choose does not mean that all of my decisions will have positive outcomes. As women, we must learn that who we are and what we give is a gift, in the same way, men have to also view their bodies as valuable and sacred. We see it every day. You will have a woman or a man who has created boundaries to maintain their purity, but because the other person hasn't, temptation comes and tries to tear down those walls; sometimes succeeding.

If we as women (young and old) honored our bodies and if men (young and old) viewed themselves as leaders and as a prized possession, both would be able to enjoy the beauty of all things, not just good, but perfect in His time. It's not about how "that guy" makes you feel. Often it's about what you don't feel independently from that guy. You know the interesting thing about Creation is that Adam did not ask for Eve. He was busy doing what God created him to do. God looked at Adam and at all of Creation and decided that something was missing that Adam needed, it was a woman. So you see, when we are being chased down by men (no matter the age), it's not because of what we are wearing or how long our hair may be. It's because sometimes that man has not found his purpose or has become disinterested in his purpose that he is looking for you as a distraction. Think about it, Adam was so busy doing what God had called him to do, that God had to literally put him to sleep to give him Eve. He wasn't bored with his life or aimlessly searching. He was productive, working, and being complete in God. Now, on the other hand, ladies; if that guy in your life does not have time for you, it only means that God has not put him to sleep yet, or simply, you are not his Eve! Adam didn't wake up and ask God "Who is she or why is she in my life." He woke up knowing I am for her, and she is for me! God is all about our lives being correctly positioned partnerships!

No matter what you do, a man will not wake up to a voice that he was not created to identify or know. As women of all ages, we must respect ourselves and respect our brothers enough to wait in the back seat with our seat belt on and our clothes! Taking matters into our own hands will lead to hurt, pain, embarrassment, shame, and more importantly, disconnect from God. God has a plan, and His plan is perfect. When we begin to consider ourselves to be the jewels and treasured girls/women that we are, our way of communicating with our counterparts will look a lot different. In fact, it will look more like God's way and less like ours. I challenge you throughout this chapter to write a list of who you believe God to send, but also a list of who you desire to be for the glory of God and for the right type of man that you are praying for. There is nothing like wanting what we have not been prepared for. What good is it, to have something in our possession that we will lose because we didn't follow instructions concerning maintenance at some point?

After my first relationship had ended as according to God's plan, I met a man that I just knew, (I was convinced, that I was going to make him "the one." Sound familiar?) would someday be my husband. We spent 9 years together; loving each other, arguing with each other, and a whole lot of convincing ourselves that after years and years of investing in this type of commitment, we would certainly not walk away from each other. We did everything we knew to do. We prayed. We talked. We prayed some more and argued some more. The truth is, we had become so complacent with each other that we couldn't see how unhealthy we were making each other. It's true, you can love someone into an unhealthy state by not allowing them to walk away. Now, I'm going to be honest with you. I loved him so much that I was willing to remind him of who I was. I was his "Eve" and after all of these years, I felt that I had the right to remind him. I couldn't have been more wrong. I remember God taking me to Genesis and having me read about Adam's posture when he woke up to Eve and interestingly enough, I observed that never once did Eve have to explain who she was.

Needless to say, my efforts didn't result in anything but brokenness. When we try to take on a role that God has not given to us, and that God has not led a man to make (no matter the time of investment), what we are doing is trying to claim a role that doesn't belong to us. I have to tell you that I have never experienced brokenness that had me second guess my worth and value, like what I experienced in trying to take a role that had not been given. My sister, this journey of pursuing purity is much bigger than sex. I'm talking about a state of mind and also a state of our intentions. I felt that my heart was in the right place over those nine years, but when we have not submitted our desires to God, our desires become just that; ours. I had to quickly learn that if I wanted to experience real freedom and to continually live a life of purity, I would also need God to clean my heart of every thought that was not of Him.

I would be lying to you if I didn't tell you that I had intense moments of grief that I never thought would be a part of my journey. But, when you allow God to do what only He can do, He reveals matters of the heart. While we may have shared the same personal convictions concerning our purity, there were certain doors open that awakened an artificial sense of love and appreciation. This is why it's important to establish boundaries before and during a relationship. The consistency of thought and frequent conversations are the only way to remain pure in heart, mind, and deed. And can we prove the devil to be a liar today, it doesn't matter if you are engaged or you think that you know without a shadow of a doubt that this will be your husband. If your last name has not changed, your interaction with one another should honor the fact that you are not his wife, and he is not your husband. The beauty of intimacy is to be enjoyed between a man and a woman that have committed to honor and love each other in the established covenant of holy matrimony.

You see, we often talk about fornication (sex before marriage) but very rarely speak of the doors that are opened to lust just in conversations and forms of entertainment such as movies and music. When we allow ourselves to be entertained (opened) to concepts and themes that are created out of intimacy, shared among people who are not married, the idea of impurity enters into our minds. We may not always see it right away, but sooner or later feelings will come, and distractions will come. Then dreams will come that have been created because of the doors that have been opened. For example, have you ever had an explicit dream and found yourself disturbed and confused concerning where it came from? I'm sure you have, at least once. But if you haven't, I give honor and praise to God for you and pray that you would continually guard your heart, your life, your eyes, and your ears because the enemy looks for anything that would give him an open invitation.

I often share my personal journey of freedom from lust (sexual desires that derive from improper and premature seasons of our lives, completely self-driven and often self-centered) and also freedom from looking for a relationship to complete "the picture." Though I am a virgin, I struggled with lust in various ways such a masturbation, movies, and also music. Yes, you can struggle with lust even while being a virgin because lust is a perverted spirit that attaches to anything that we allow in our lives that have been created for marriage only. I recall seeing, as a child, a sexual encounter and seeing movies that had sexual content. Some years ago God literally freed me from it all including masturbation. In all honesty, God took that desire away. I kid you not. To this day I can't remember the last time that lust was a struggle. I say that not to make you feel bad if it is still a struggle for you, but to demonstrate the power of God at work. God can free you if you truly desire to be free and to live a pure life.

I have found that when we hide, we remain broken. But when we reveal that which has been hidden, God then brings healing to our hearts and our bodies. Understanding your personal worth and value plays a significant role in understanding who you are in Christ. When you don't understand who you are, your actions will follow suit with that. I began to realize that my value and what I would one day be able to offer my husband (when God wakes him up) was far more precious and valuable than self-pleasure (sin). I began to understand that what I was doing was robbing myself, as well as my future husband, from the gift of becoming one and experiencing intimacy with him in the way God had intended.

My personal journey of freedom did not begin because I wanted to be free, but because I needed to be free. There is a difference between being a virgin and living a pure life. I have many friends who are not virgins but have made solid commitments to God to live a life of purity. I also have friends and at one point myself, struggled with impurity though I was a virgin. So abstaining from sexual encounters does not mean that you have reached an ultimate level of what God desires. Unless you are pursuing a life that not only abstains from sexual pleasure but also strives toward complete freedom and purity in action, conversation, and even various forms of entertainment, you will be open for attack. I learned that the hard way. I was convinced that I was better than my friends who were having sex because I thought at least this is something that I'm not doing with a guy. I am thankful that God stopped me in my tracks and said, "Miracle, you may be a virgin, but you are not pure right now." This hit me like a ton of bricks. I remember crying out to God and I also remember sharing with people what God had done and about the freedom that came. What a transformation of the mind!

If you are currently in a lifestyle that is not pure, I encourage you to email me at *mtreed86@gmail.com*. I would love to help you walk through the process and your ongoing journey to freedom. Everything that you share remains confidential and even, at some point, you would like to have a phone conversation, I am open to that as well. I understand how difficult it is, but I also know the incredible joy and love that has come with being completely free from lust and looking forward to one day being able to share myself completely with my future husband. This is not an easy journey, but it can become a part of your life the moment you surrender. Having people in your life who you can trust and who will hold you accountable is important. But so is filtering what you watch and also setting clear boundaries from the first dates that you have.

Don't trick people because you are afraid of what they may say or do. Stand up for yourself and place all of your "goods" on lock until you can give your all in marriage. There is freedom for you, my sister, and there is continual power and grace for whoever does not struggle in this area. God loves us so much and when we fully understand His love we are then then able to comprehend what love is not. No matter what you have given away, God can restore and make you whole again. I have friends who have children that have made a stance of purity and refuse to use their pregnancy as a means to continue in sin. This means that no one has an excuse.

Faith without works is dead and in the same way, freedom without consistent action to remain free is dead as well. There is no way that we can live a pure life while entertaining things and situations that have the potential to fall. The Bible says in 2 Timothy 2:22 "Run from anything that stimulates youthful lusts. Instead, pursue righteous living, faithfulness, love, and peace. Enjoy the companionship of those who call on the Lord with pure hearts." Do you know what this means in today's world? Allow me to share with you just a few practical steps that would keep us away from things that stimulate youthful desires. But first, understand that the reason why it says "youthful" desires is because youth often tends to make decisions without thinking of the consequences or results that sometimes do not appear until much later.

You see, what is being conveyed in 2 Timothy is to not merely run from sex or things that lead to sex. Rather, Paul is encouraging Timothy to run from the behaviors and patterns of this world that cause you to embrace the temporary lustful satisfactions, without recognizing the long-term consequences (which often take the form of brokenness, low self-esteem, and regret). There are life-long results that are carried with us from our first impure encounter well into our adult years. Sure, we may not see them or feel them right away but, at some point, it catches up with us because of the void that remains unfilled.

The Purity Pledge

Practical Steps to Remain Pure

- Study the Word of God regarding purity, worth, value, as well as image. Also, look at accounts that talk about what happens when you fall into lust (i.e. Samson, David, Woman at the well, etc.).

- Be honest concerning your boundaries and limits.

- Do not press those boundaries and limits. Everyone knows how far is too far.

  o *Tips: Keep clothes on at all times; do not stay the night; consider the content of movies during dates and while alone. Maintain boundaries in conversations, and be modest in apparel. (Men, no matter their age, are visual beings. Protect their mind and their eyes in any way that you can.) Keep the following scripture in mind. This is God's will for us!

- 1 Thessalonians 4:3-5, "God's will is for you to be holy, so stay away from all sexual sin. Then each of you will control his own body and live in holiness and honor— not in lustful passion like the pagans who do not know God and his ways." (NLT)

- Have people in your life who will hold you accountable.

- When you feel vulnerable, spend that time in prayer. Seriously, the enemy knows when we are weak spiritually. The worst thing you could do is call up the guy because chances are, that void you feel will be artificially filled.

- Don't listen to music that takes your mind to a place that is meant to be enjoyed within marriage.

These are only a few practical steps that can play a significant role in your efforts to remain pure before the Lord. It is my prayer that you not only know your worth and how precious your body is but that you also understand the worth and value of the male interests that you have in your life. It's not enough for me to tell you that you are a gift without reminding you that your brothers in Christ are gifts as well. Purity is not reserved for women alone, God desires this for His sons and daughters alike. And I will tell you, my sister, there is nothing like meeting an amazingly attractive man and hearing his testimony about his pursuit of purity! Whew, yes Lord! I say that because when a man makes a decision to remain pure or to commit to a pure life until marriage, it speaks volumes about how he will love, honor, and respect you. If he does it before he has you, he will certainly do it after.

Are you ready to take the pledge? The pledge that will change the way you allow yourself to be pursued, the way you dress, and the way you think about yourself. Here we go!

I declare that I am a daughter of the King and that my body is to be honored as a temple where the Holy Spirit dwells. I will not lower my standards to meet the approval, or counterfeit love that I know can only be given by God. I pledge to wait for God to wake up my "Adam" revealing to him that I am his Eve. I will not rush the process or journey, but I will remain patient no matter my age or the relationship goals that are being created through social media. My life is to be a reflection of God's love and relentless pursuit, and I will not settle for anything less. I understand and take full responsibility for the role that I have in honoring my body in what I say, how I dress, what I watch, and things that I do. I do not blame anyone for things that I've done but neither will I live in regret because I am now free. I declare that purity is not identified only in what I do but also in who I am and who I become. I desire to have a pure heart, and I thank you, Father, for removing everything in me that doesn't look like you. From this day forward, I pledge and commit to living a pure life and being held accountable by people who I trust and who are serving you. This is my life, a life of purity. In Jesus' name, Amen.

My sister, at this moment I give God praise for what you have done. You have no idea what this means and how your decision will inspire friends and even guys that become interested in you. I've learned over the years that leadership has to start with someone and that someone is always the person that decides to take the first step. I don't know where the person may be in your life right now or the people that you will meet along this journey, but I encourage you in your decision, to put one foot in front of the other and keep following God. I also want to urge you to know when it is time to stop and take a stand for what you know is right. As I mentioned, feel free to email me with any comments, questions, or hardships that you may face along the path. I am more than willing to interact with you, and I am making myself available. I honestly believe that this is what life is all about!

No matter what your yesterday looked like, know that you serve a God, who loves you unconditionally and will never leave you. There will be days of temptation, there will be moments of weakness, but remember that God's strength is made perfect in your weakness. There is nothing that you will have to go through alone, and there is no darkness that can keep the light of Christ from shining through. Your "yes" and your decision to surrender to Christ is that light that shines through that darkness. Keep going, God isn't done with you yet. You are and will forever be "Daddy's Little Girl."

Purity is not just a way to live your life. It is a way of thinking, speaking, doing, and being. Purity is life.

CHAPTER 14

Daddy's Little Girl

"See what great love the Father has lavished on us,
that we should be called children of God! And that is
what we are! The reason the world does not know us
is that it did not know him." 1 John 3:1 (NIV)

Every girl loves daddy-daughter time. A time where she can sit on daddy's lap and make her requests known. In this same manner, our Heavenly Father desires for us to rest in Him. He wants to have quiet time with us, seeing what's in our hearts and hearing about the things we feel have been forgotten. There is nothing like having one-on-one time with the Father and basking in His presence, soaking in His goodness. For me, during the summer, He and I have what I call "dates in the park." These are moments that I cherish with God alone. Most of the time I don't invite people to come with me. I simply bask in His presence with the Son and sun shining down on me.

As Daughters of the King, I challenge and encourage you to create an environment that is peaceful with just you and God. He loves you so much, and what you gain in just a day with God, you could spend your entire life searching for. You see, our understanding of worth and value comes mostly from our parents and what it was considered to be as children. We also understand our worth and value by what we are told and what is modeled before us. This would be the perfect way to learn our value if we lived in a perfect world. But because some of us come from broken homes, dysfunctional backgrounds, and single-parent families, we often didn't see what we should have, heard what we needed, or experienced what every daughter should have.

However, God knew that there would be many of us who would not get what we needed from our earthly parents, so He came declaring that we have all been adopted as His sons and daughters (Ephesians 1:5). In fact, God desires to love you with a love that can never be replaced or taken away. I affirm you as a Daughter of the Most-High, declaring that your worth and value is far greater than what you could ever imagine and more valuable than what the eye can see. You have been through a lot, but you are still here. The amazing thing about you is that you have lived to tell it! People counted you out, you may even have counted yourself out, and often people tried to take you out but look at what God has done. He calls you Daughter, He calls you

His precious and most prized possession, not as an owner would call his property, but as a father would as he looks at what has been created of himself.

There have been many things that you have endured, and when God looks at you, He sees a reflection of Himself. You belong to God and just as 1 John 3 states, the reason people do not fully know or understand you is because you are not of this world. You belong to Christ. You have been set aside and appointed for greatness. This means you have no limitations in God. *The only limitations you have are the ones that you create for yourself.* Matthew 6:8 reminds us that our Father knows what we need, again showing us that there is no lack in Him. Wherever you are right now and whatever you have been reminded of throughout this book, remember that no matter who tries to limit you, God will not.

When we seek God above all else, we become perfectly aligned with all the plans that God has for us. There is nothing that God will not do for you. He loves you and all of the things that you tell him while you sit on His lap, know that He is indeed listening. My sister, please know that you are so precious to God, and there is nothing that will ever snatch you away from Him! From this day forward, it is my continual prayer that you would see the greatness, the treasure, the jewel that you are in this world. What you add to this world according to Matthew 5:13 is salt, which means you are the one to give the world its flavor. You, as a Daughter of the King, have the ability to set the stage and create the environment that you desire.

Never let someone make you feel like your goals or aspirations are unattainable. You are a Daughter of the King, and your worth and value are not measured by what you do, it is always measured by who you are in Christ. Living each day according to God's purpose is more than just praying and reading the Bible, it is living out your faith daily in how you love people. "Don't just pretend to love others. Really love them. Hate what is wrong. Hold tightly to what is good. Love each other with genuine affection, and take delight in honoring each other" (Romans 12:9-10). This is what God desires; for us to love authentically and for us to literally hate that which is wrong. People will know that we belong to God, not because we read the Bible every day, but because they see the love of Jesus shining in and through us as we love others.

The concept of being "Daddy's Little Girl" makes me feel incredibly special because although God has restored the relationship between my dad and I, but I have a relationship with my Heavenly Father that has established the foundation of my identity. I've spent many nights feeling alone and often unimportant because of my family struggles during my childhood. But now, I can honestly say that in every moment, God gave me hope that it would not always be that way. I stand before you today as an example that it doesn't matter what you've gone through or what you have been stuck in; God loves you and will use you for His glory wherever you may be. I tell you that God will make up for what you didn't have. He will do what no one else can and give you peace beyond measure.

Being my Heavenly Father's little girl reminds me that no matter what I accomplish and the numbers that increase with age, I will always be "Daddy's Little Girl." If you have ever felt the love of God bring warmth and comfort to your heart, then you know exactly what I mean. There is nothing that compares to the love of the Father. I encourage you to steal away time for just you and God daily. You will be surprised by the impact that one day can have on your entire life. "Better is one day in your courts than a thousand elsewhere. I would rather be a doorkeeper in the house of my God than dwell in the tents of the wicked" Psalm 84:10 (NIV).

It is my prayer that you are encouraged by what you have read, declared, and released. There is nothing and no one that can hold you back. You are free in Him; you are made new in Him, and you are whole. My sister, you are a beautiful image bearer of Christ and who you are in Him is far greater than who you will ever be to the world. Never limit who you are to fit inside of a box that God created you to live outside of. There will be days where that box will look quite comfortable and even tempting, but in those moments remind yourself that not only are you "Daddy's little Girl," you are treasured and worth far more than the inside of that box can provide!

Live your life in anticipation of what God has in store for you and for those who you are connected to. Pass this book on to your girlfriends and family members, maybe even use it as a group study! Whatever you do, don't keep it to yourself! In the same way we share the details of the new sale taking place at our favorite store, let's also extend to those we love an invitation to a life that will be far more valuable when lived in Christ and in purity.

God has wiped the tears that have followed you throughout your life. He has carried you through obstacles that you thought you would never get through, and He has given you a new name for all of the world to see that you are truly treasured by the King.

A Message of Empowerment

To

The Single Woman, The Teenage Girl, The Wife, and The Mother

The most beautiful things in life have always been the things not readily available. Think of what life would look like if everything of great worth sat on a counter for all to see, touch, take, or own. The concept of value would be nothing more than our personal views or interests. If everything of worth was readily available, there would no longer be a scale to measure what we could or could not afford. There would be no need for a pursuit of anything or the need to maintain what has been attained. However, Jesus comes on the scene introducing a life of great significance and value that has been hidden in Him (Colossians 3:1-4). It is no wonder why there is such a fight and a struggle to maintain our identity in Christ. The enemy is quite aware that when we start to truly walk in the reality of who we are in Him, there is no stopping us. But because he knows our areas of vulnerability due to doors we've opened in our lives he lurks in the shadow of them, like the thief that he is.

The plan of the enemy is to devalue us to the point of thinking that the ultimate satisfaction in life is to have the role as a wife, have children, or become owners of some sort. However, in and of itself, there is nothing wrong with any of those things, but when we choose to live our lives in search of what will never bring complete fulfillment, we rob ourselves of the beauty of the life that is hidden in Christ. As a minister and one who provides counseling for both single and married women, I have come to find that when we are not rooted in the reality of who we are before marriage, family, or a job. We either identify ourselves based on what we have (family, spouse, job) or devalue ourselves, based on what we don't have. This is the danger of not knowing who you are in Christ. When this happens, you end up trying to re-identify yourself by that which is surface and conditional.

Now, while I have had the incredible honor to be a part of the special day of many of my close girlfriends; I am quite aware that what is accomplished with "I do" is maintained with "I do again and again." The reality is that what we desire the most is hidden beneath the depth of a daily decision of selflessness; whether single or married. When we forget that our joy, peace, and contentment is a daily decision, we will always find ourselves looking outward instead of looking within. There is no magic to joy in this life. There is but one answer and one method; daily choosing Him before He sends you him (your soulmate), it, or them. In this season of your life, wherever that may be, know that your past, present, and future is being held in the palm of God's hand. All God requires from you is a selfless "yes" to kickstart the healing and the journey He has planned for you specifically.

When you looked at the cover of this book, not only did you see the title, but you saw a beautiful pearl that was hidden within a clam. Not only is the pearl hidden inside of the clam, but it was created inside the clam as well. What a beautiful picture of what God does with us. While we desire to be seen, acknowledged, loved, admired and appreciated; we have a God, who loves us so much that He doesn't reveal us to the world until He has beautified us from within. There is a process that we must all go through, either willingly and gracefully, or kicking and screaming. This process is being made whole and complete. Now, I know you may be thinking, "Miracle, I see what you are saying, but I'm 48, complete, married with a family; recently graduated from high school; just came back from our honeymoon." The truth is that nothing you accomplish in this world will bring you wholeness.

It is only in the posture of complete surrender that we find complete wholeness in Christ. This is how I am knocking on 30 doors rather quickly, without concern, worry, or doubt about marriage, having a family, or owning a home. God has given me complete contentment and joy in Him. You see, when we truly know who we are in God, it no longer becomes a concern of who we are not in the world. I will be honest with you. When I meet people, either before I preach, speak at an event, or host a program, one of the first questions that I'm asked is if I'm married. It's almost as if people (both men and women) look at me and wonder how I do what I'm doing, whether it's traveling, preaching, or kayaking without a partner. I share this with you because I never find the question offensive. It always becomes an opportunity for me to reflect on the reality that the greatest life that could ever be lived is life in the will of God.

I remember wanting what everyone else had, but then I started providing counseling; only to find that most of the women I counsel wanted what I had. *We are very quick to discredit or underestimate the value of where we are when we do not see the worth and value of where God has brought us from.* It is no different for the single woman who is looking at the married woman, or the married woman looking at the mother. When we do not have peace and contentment where we are, we will always desire to be somewhere else. But, my sisters, today allow me to remind you, that you are right where God wants you. He made NO mistakes with the portion that He has given you, and He has not turned a deaf ear to what you desire. Life is not about what you thought you should have or where you thought you should be. It's about loving every season you find yourself in and having joy in the midst of it.

I just love how Nehemiah reminds us that our joy is not from where we are, who we have, or what we've accomplished. Our joy is rooted in the reality of the consistency of God. When we look for that boyfriend, husband, son/daughter, or job to be our source of joy, we limit ourselves, and we limit God. *God never intended for His blessings to be the source of our joy. He intended for the blessings to continually point us back to Him as the source (not an option) of our joy.* You may be experiencing the sweetest season of your life as a single girl/woman. You may be having the time of your life with your husband, or your children may have recently brought home straight A's. However, if these temporary seasons of your life have the ability to alter your view of the season that you are in, you have missed the whole point. God's plan for His daughters is to live each day blown away by the beauty of God's plan.

When we stop looking at the beauty of His plan and start focusing on the disappointment of ours, we have fallen into the trap of *The Lie of Limit in the Midst of Abundance* (you can read more about this in my book *When God Vetoes Your Plan*).

If there is an area of lack in your life, it's not because God has kept something from you; it's because you have limited yourself by welcoming artificial fillers in your life (people, places, or things that only have the ability to bring temporary satisfaction). So, I say to you today, embrace where you are, enjoy where you are and be reminded that God knows what you need. Also, never question that God also knows how and when you need it. Be empowered in the reality that your worst days have come and gone, and you are still standing. That relationship did not break you; that class did not stop you; your children did not hinder you, and even the thoughts that you have had about yourself could not keep you from experiencing God. Daughters of the King, you have made it and what God is getting ready to release into your life, into your hands, and into your families a daily reminder of who you are. You are **Treasured**, a rare and unique gift that God has placed, not on the shelf to collect dust, but behind the glass to be polished and shined daily. You are indeed a Daughter of the King.

SPECIAL THANKS

To

The Treasured Girls of Prince George, BC, Canada:

Alexis McMordie
Anna McIvor
Kathy Davis
Kristy Houston-McMillan
Natasha Jang
Madison Schultz
Rose Hope

I AM TREASURED DECLARATION

"I declare that I am a Daughter of the King. My worth and value are not measured by what I've accomplished, but by the content of my character. I am treasured, and I am far more valuable than what the eye can see. My life is hidden in Christ, and my heart is held in His hands. I will not compromise my love for Christ to establish superficial friendships, relationships, or status. I was born to stand out, so I refuse to fit in. May my life be a billboard for all the world to see that I am treasured by the KING.

CONNECT WITH MIRACLE:

Social Media

Facebook.com/miracle.reed/
Twitter @MiracleReed
Instagram: Iammissmiracle

Email:connectwithmiracle@gmail.com

**For more information or booking visit
www.miraclereed.com**

About Miracle

Miracle Reed is a native of Pittsburgh, Pennsylvania and has been committed to serving God since 1996. It was certainly apparent from the very beginning that her life would be an inspiration to many. She was born three months premature, weighing 1.6 pounds at birth, placing her in the twentieth percentile of babies who survive weighing a little over a pound. Not only did the Great Physician take over, but He also allowed the life of one to prove to all those who would meet her that nothing is impossible with God. It is no wonder why her name is Miracle!

Miracle is the daughter of parents that have struggled with drug addiction. This gives her a platform to stand tall as an advocate of hope and inspiration for people who have been challenged with this same storm. She provides and presents "the way" for people, in seeing first-hand a process of freedom within the lives of her own parents. People often wonder how she managed to accomplish all that she has, while experiencing great turmoil, neglect, and confusion. She often responds with, "I knew from the time I was a child that I could either feel alone, live in sorrow and anger or I could become empowered by every experience, building a bridge of hope for others, while creating one for myself. I chose the latter."

Her obedience, passion, and love for God have given her the opportunities to not only preach, appear on television and newspapers, but counsel and pastor not only in the United States, but the Caribbean, and Canada as well. Miracle believes the only limit in life is that which we create. We must become open to God without restraints to truly live without limits. She is living proof of how there are no boundaries when God is in control. It is her desire to live a life inspiring others to welcome the plan of God and experience the beauty of a life devoted to Him.

Miracle is a graduate of the Marilyn J. Davis School of the Bible, where she received her license for ministry as well as a diploma in the Bible. She also graduated from Geneva College, where she received bachelor's degrees in both Biblical Studies and Human Services. She has created ministry discipleship programs and workshops designed to bring forth healing, complete wholeness, family restoration, and inspiration. She is the author of *When God Vetoes Your Plan* and *Living Out Loud in a Silent World* as well as the creator of the *Why Me/Yes You* discipleship course. She has also recently started MRInc, LLC, a small company that provides ministry development consultation, leadership workshops, individual spiritual growth and development counseling, and much more. Miracle loves God and has a passion for fulfilling His plan above all things. She lives each day humbled by the opportunities of being a part of that plan.

Miracle currently travels the world sharing the love of Jesus and a message of empowerment, hope, and joy in churches, universities, and various organizations.

OTHER TITLES BY MIRACLE

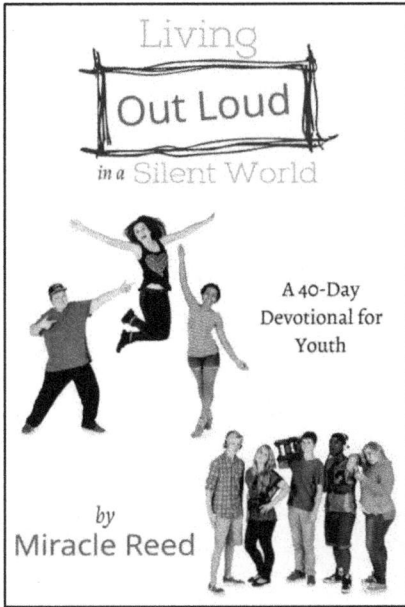

Living Out Loud in a Silent World

A 40-Day Devotional for Youth

by Miracle Reed

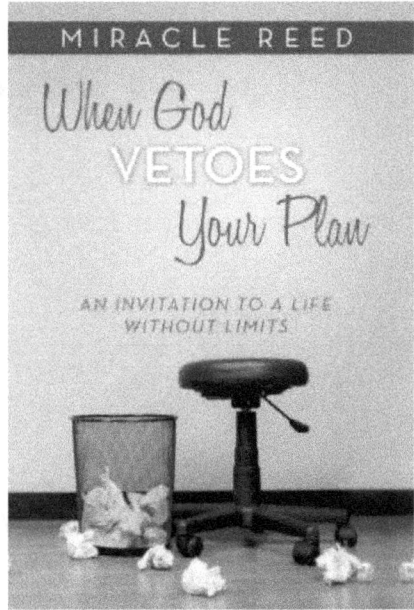

MIRACLE REED

When God VETOES Your Plan

AN INVITATION TO A LIFE WITHOUT LIMITS

Available on Amazon.com and Barnes & Noble

www.ingramcontent.com/pod-product-compliance
Lightning Source LLC
Chambersburg PA
CBHW020906100426

42737CB00044B/392